ESSAYS

By

DAVID HUME

With Biographical Introduction

by

Hannaford Bennett

David Hume

1711–1776

Contents

Biographical Introduction

Of The Delicacy Of Taste And Passion

Of The Liberty Of The Press

That Politics May Be Reduced To A Science

Of The First Principles Of Government

Of The Origin Of Government

Of The Independency Of Parliament

Whether The British Government Inclines More To Absolute Monarchy Or To A Republic

Of Parties In General

Of The Parties Of Great Britain

Of Superstition And Enthusiasm

Of The Dignity Or Meanness Of Human Nature

Of Civil Liberty

Of Eloquence

Biographical Introduction

The material facts in Hume's life are to be found in the autobiography which he prefixed to his *History of England*. *My Own Life*, as he calls it, is but a brief exposition, but it is sufficient for its purpose, and the longer biographies of him do little more than amplify the information which he gives us himself. The Humes, it appears, were a remote branch of the family of Lord Hume of Douglas. Hume's father was Joseph Hume, of Ninewells, a minor Scotch laird, who died when his son was an infant. David Hume was born at Edinburgh on April 26th, 1711, during a visit of his parents to the Scotch capital. Hume tells us that his father passed for a man of parts, and that his mother, who herself came of good Scottish family, "was a woman of singular merit; though young and handsome, she devoted herself entirely to the rearing and educating of her children." At school Hume won no special distinction. He matriculated in the class of Greek at the Edinburgh University when he was twelve years old, and, he says "passed through the ordinary course of education with success"; but "our college education in Scotland," he remarks in one of his works, "extending little further than the languages, ends commonly when we are about fourteen or fifteen years of age." During his youth, Mrs. Hume does not appear to have maintained any too flattering opinion of her son's abilities; she considered him a good-natured but "uncommon weak-minded" creature. Possibly her judgment underwent a change in course of time, since she lived to see the beginnings of his literary fame; but his worldly success was long in the making, and he was a middle-aged man before his meagre fortune was converted into anything like a decent maintenance.

It may have been Hume's apparent vacillation in choosing a career that made this "shrewd Scots wife" hold her son in such small esteem. At first the family tried to launch him into the profession of the law, but "while they fancied I was poring over Voet and Vinnius, Cicero and Virgil were the authors I was secretly devouring." For six years Hume remained at Ninewells and then made "a feeble trial for entering on a more active scene of life." Commerce, this time, was the chosen instrument, but the result was not more successful. "In 1734 I went to Bristol with some recommendations to eminent merchants, but in a few months found that scene totally unsuitable for me." At length—in the middle of 1736 when Hume was twenty-three years of age and without any profession or means of earning a livelihood—he went over to France. He settled first at Rheims, and afterwards at La Flêche in Anjou, and "there I laid that plan of life which I have steadily and successfully pursued. I resolved to make a very rigid frugality supply my deficiency of fortune, to maintain unimpaired my independency, and to regard every object as contemptible except the improvement of my talents in literature." At La Flêche Hume lived in frequent intercourse with the Jesuits at the famous college in which Descartes was educated, and he composed his first book, the *Treatise of Human Nature*. According to himself "it fell dead-born from the press, without reaching such distinction as even to excite a murmur among the zealots." But this work which was planned before the author was twenty-one and written before he was twenty-five, in the opinion of Professor Huxley, is probably the most remarkable philosophical work, both intrinsically and in its effects upon the course of thought, that has ever been written. Three years later Hume published anonymously, at Edinburgh, the first volume of *Essays, Moral and Political*, which was followed in 1742 by the second volume. The *Essays*, he says, were favourably received and soon made me entirely forget my former disappointments.

In 1745 Hume became tutor to a young nobleman, the Marquis of Annandale, who was mentally affected, but he did not endure the engagement for long. Next year General St. Clair, who had been appointed to command an expedition in the War of the Pragmatic Sanction, invited him to be his secretary, an office to which that of judge-advocate was afterwards added. The expedition was a failure, but General St. Clair, who was afterwards entrusted with embassies to Turin and Vienna, and upon whom Hume seems to have created a favourable impression, insisted that he should accompany him in the same capacity as secretary; he further made him one of his *aides-de-camp*. Thus Hume had to attire his portly figure in a "scarlet military uniform," and Lord Charlemont who met him in Turin says that he wore his uniform "like a grocer of the train-bands." At Vienna the Empress-Dowager excused him on ceremonial occasions from walking backwards, a concession which was much appreciated by "my companions who were desperately afraid of my falling on them and crushing them." Hume returned to London in 1749. "These years," he says, "were almost the only interruptions my studies have received during the course of my life. I passed them agreeably and in good company, and my appointments, with my frugality, had made me reach a fortune which I called independent, though most of my friends were inclined to smile when I said so; in short, I was now master of near a thousand pounds."

While Hume was away with General St. Clair his *Inquiry Concerning Human Understanding* was published, but it was not more successful than the original *Treatise* of a portion of which it was a recasting. A new edition of *Moral and Political Essays* met with no better fate, but these disappointments, he says, "made little or no impression" on him. In 1749 Hume returned to Ninewells, and lived for a while with his brothers. Afterwards he took a flat of his own at Edinburgh, with his sister to keep house for him. At this period the *Political Discourses* and the *Inquiry concerning the Principles of Morals* were published. Of the *Inquiry* Hume held the opinion, an opinion, however, which was not shared by the critics, that "it is of all my writings—historical, philosophical, or literary incomparably the best." Slowly and surely his publications were growing in reputation. In 1752 the Faculty of Advocates elected Hume their librarian, an office which was valuable to him, not so much for the emolument as for the extensive library which enabled him to pursue the historical studies upon which he had for some time been engaged. For the next nine years he was occupied with his *History of England*. The first volume was published in 1754, and the second volume, which met with a better reception than the first, in 1756. Only forty-five copies of the first volume were sold in a twelvemonth; but the subsequent volumes made rapid headway, and raised a great clamour, for in the words of Macaulay, Hume's historical picture, though drawn by a master hand, has all the lights Tory and all the shades Whig. In 1757 one of his most remarkable works, the *Natural History of Religion*, appeared. The book was attacked—not wholly to Hume's dissatisfaction, for he appreciated fame as well as success—"with all the illiberal petulance, arrogance, and scurrility which distinguish the Warburtonian school."

Hume remained in Edinburgh superintending the publication of the *History* until 1763 when Lord Hertford, who had been appointed ambassador to France, offered him office in the embassy, with the promise of the secretaryship later on. The appointment was the more honourable, inasmuch as Hume was not personally acquainted with Lord Hertford, who had a reputation for virtue and piety, whilst Hume's views about religion had rendered him one of the best abused men of his time. In France Hume's reputation stood higher than it was in England; several of his works had been translated into French; and he had corresponded with Montesquieu, Helvetius and Rousseau. Thus he was received in French society with every mark of distinction. In a letter to Adam Smith in October 1763, he wrote: "I have been three days at Paris and two at Fontainebleau, and have everywhere met with the most extraordinary honours, which the most exorbitant vanity could wish or desire." Great nobles fêted him, and great ladies struggled for the presence of the "*gros David*" at their receptions or in their boxes at the theatre. "At the opera his broad unmeaning face was usually to be seen *entre deux joli minois*," says Lord Charlemont. Hume took his honours with satisfaction, but with becoming good sense, and he did not allow these flatteries to turn his head.

In 1767 Hume was back in London, and for the next two years held office as Under-Secretary of State. It is not necessary to dwell upon this period of his life, or to go into the details of his quarrel with Rousseau. In 1769 he returned to Edinburgh "very opulent" in the possession of £1,000 a year, and determined to take the rest of his life easily and pleasantly. He built himself a house in Edinburgh, and for the next six years it was the centre of the most accomplished society in the city. In 1755 Hume's health began to fail, and he knew that his illness must be fatal. Thus he made his will and wrote *My Own Life*, which ends simply in these words:

"I now reckon upon a speedy dissolution. I have suffered very little pain from my disorder; and what is more strange have, notwithstanding the great decline of my person, never suffered a moment's abatement of spirits; insomuch that were I to name the period of my life which I should most choose to pass over again, I might be tempted to point to this later period. I possess the same ardour as ever in study, and the same gaiety in company; I consider, besides, that a man of sixty-five, by dying, cuts off only a few years of infirmities; and though I see many symptoms of my literary reputation's breaking out at last with additional lustre, I know that I could have but few years to enjoy it. It is difficult to be more detached from life than I am at present.

"To conclude historically with my own character, I am, or rather was (for that is the style I must now use in speaking of myself); I was, I say, a man of mild dispositions, of command of temper, of an open, social, and cheerful humour, capable of attachment, but little susceptible of enmity, and of great moderation in all my passions. Even my love of literary fame, my ruling passion, never soured my temper, notwithstanding my frequent disappointments. My company was not unacceptable to the young and careless, as well as to the studious and literary; and as I took a particular pleasure in the company of modest women, I had no reason to be displeased with the reception I met with from them. In a word, though most men any wise eminent, have found reason to complain of calumny, I never was touched or even attacked by her baleful tooth; and though I wantonly exposed myself to the rage of both civil and religious factions, they seemed to be disarmed in my behalf of their wonted fury.

My friends never had occasion to vindicate any one circumstance of my character and conduct; not but that the zealots, we may well suppose, would have been glad to invent and propagate any story to my disadvantage, but they could never find any which they thought would wear the face of probability. I cannot say there is no vanity in making this funeral oration of myself, but I hope it is not a misplaced one; and this is a matter of fact which is easily cleared and ascertained."

Hume died in Edinburgh on August 25th, 1776, and a few days later was buried in a spot selected by himself on the Carlton Hill.

HANNAFORD BENNETT

OF THE DELICACY OF TASTE AND PASSION

Some people are subject to a certain *delicacy* of *passion*, which makes them extremely sensible to all the accidents of life, and gives them a lively joy upon every prosperous event, as well as a piercing grief when they meet with misfortune and adversity. Favours and good offices easily engage their friendship, while the smallest injury provokes their resentment. Any honour or mark of distinction elevates them above measure, but they are sensibly touched with contempt. People of this character have, no doubt, more lively enjoyments, as well as more pungent sorrows, than men of cool and sedate tempers. But, I believe, when every thing is balanced, there is no one who would not rather be of the latter character, were he entirely master of his own disposition. Good or ill fortune is very little at our disposal; and when a person that has this sensibility of temper meets with any misfortune, his sorrow or resentment takes entire possession of him, and deprives him of all relish in the common occurrences of life, the right enjoyment of which forms the chief part of our happiness. Great pleasures are much less frequent than great pains, so that a sensible temper must meet with, fewer trials in the former way than in the latter. Not to mention, that men of such lively passions are apt to be transported beyond all bounds of prudence and discretion, and to take false steps in the conduct of life, which are often irretrievable.

There is a *delicacy* of *taste* observable in some men, which very much resembles this *delicacy* of *passion*, and produces the same sensibility to beauty and deformity of every kind, as that does to prosperity and adversity, obligations and injuries. When you present a poem or a picture to a man possessed of this talent, the delicacy of his feeling makes him be sensibly touched with every part of it; nor are the masterly strokes perceived with more exquisite relish and satisfaction, than the negligences or absurdities with disgust and uneasiness. A polite and judicious conversation affords him the highest entertainment; rudeness or impertinence is as great punishment to him. In short, delicacy of taste has the same effect as delicacy of passion. It enlarges the sphere both of our happiness and misery, and makes us sensible to pains as well as pleasures which escape the rest of mankind.

I believe, however, every one will agree with me, that notwithstanding this resemblance, delicacy of taste is as much to be desired and cultivated, as delicacy of passion is to be lamented, and to be remedied, if possible. The good or ill accidents of life are very little at our disposal; but we are pretty much masters what books we shall read, what diversions we shall partake of, and what company we shall keep. Philosophers have endeavoured to render happiness entirely independent of every thing external. The degree of perfection is impossible to be *attained*; but every wise man will endeavour to place his happiness on such objects chiefly as depend upon himself; and *that* is not to be *attained* so much by any other means as by this delicacy of sentiment. When a man is possessed of that talent, he is more happy by what pleases his taste, than by what gratifies his appetites, and receives more enjoyment from a poem, or a piece of reasoning, than the most expensive luxury can afford.

Whatever connection there may be originally between these two species of delicacy, I am persuaded that nothing is so proper to cure us of this delicacy of passion, as the cultivating of that higher and more refined taste, which enables us to judge of the characters of men, of the compositions of genius, and of the productions of the nobler arts. A greater or less relish for those obvious beauties which strike the senses, depends entirely upon the greater or less sensibility of the temper; but with regard to the sciences and liberal arts, a fine taste is, in some measure, the same with strong sense, or at least depends so much upon it that they are inseparable. In order to judge aright of a composition of genius, there are so many views to be taken in, so many circumstances to be compared, and such a knowledge of human nature requisite, that no man, who is not possessed of the soundest judgment, will ever make a tolerable critic in such performances. And this is a new reason for cultivating a relish in the liberal arts. Our judgment will strengthen by this exercise. We shall form juster notions of life. Many things which please or afflict others, will appear to us too frivolous to engage our attention; and we shall lose by degrees that sensibility and delicacy of passion which is so incommodious.

But perhaps I have gone too far, in saying that a cultivated taste for the polite arts extinguishes the passions, and renders us indifferent to those objects which are so fondly pursued by the rest of mankind. On further reflection, I find, that it rather improves our sensibility for all the tender and agreeable passions; at the same time that it renders the mind incapable of the rougher and more boisterous emotions.

> Ingenuas didicisse fideliter artes,
> Emollit mores, nec sinit esse feros.

For this, I think, there may be assigned two very natural reasons. In the *first* place, nothing is so improving to the temper as the study of the beauties either of poetry, eloquence, music, or painting. They give a certain elegance of sentiment to which the rest of mankind are strangers. The emotions which they excite are soft and tender. They draw off the mind from the hurry of business and interest; cherish reflection; dispose to tranquillity; and produce an agreeable melancholy, which, of all dispositions of the mind, is the best suited to love and friendship.

In the *second* place, a delicacy of taste is favourable to love and friendship, by confining our choice to few people, and making us indifferent to the company and conversation of the greater part of men. You will seldom find that mere men of the world, whatever strong sense they may be endowed with, are very nice in distinguishing characters, or in marking those insensible differences and gradations, which make one man preferable to another. Any one that has competent sense is sufficient for their entertainment. They talk to him of their pleasures and affairs, with the same frankness that they would to another; and finding many who are fit to supply his place, they never feel any vacancy or want in his absence. But to make use of the allusion of a celebrated French[1] author, the judgment may be compared to a clock or watch, where the most ordinary machine is sufficient to tell the hours; but the most elaborate alone can point out the minutes and seconds, and distinguish the smallest differences of time. One that has well digested his knowledge both of books and men, has little enjoyment but in the company of a few select companions. He feels too sensibly, how much all the rest of mankind fall short of the notions which he has entertained. And, his affections being thus confined within a narrow circle, no wonder he carries them further than if they were more general and undistinguished. The gaiety and frolic of a bottle companion improves with him into a solid friendship; and the ardours of a youthful appetite become an elegant passion.

---

[1] Mons. Fontenelle, Pluralité des Mondes, Soir 6.

OF THE LIBERTY OF THE PRESS

Nothing is more apt to surprise a foreigner, than the extreme liberty which we enjoy in this country of communicating whatever we please to the public and of openly censuring every measure entered into by the king or his ministers. If the administration resolve upon war, it is affirmed, that, either wilfully or ignorantly, they mistake the interests of the nation; and that peace, in the present situation of affairs, is infinitely preferable. If the passion of the ministers lie towards peace, our political writers breathe nothing but war and devastation, and represent the specific conduct of the government as mean and pusillanimous. As this liberty is not indulged in any other government, either republican or monarchical; in Holland and Venice, more than in France or Spain; it may very naturally give occasion to the question, *How it happens that Great Britain alone enjoys this peculiar privilege?*

The reason why the laws indulge us in such a liberty, seems to be derived from our mixed form of government, which is neither wholly monarchical, nor wholly republican. It will be found, if I mistake not, a true observation in politics, that the two extremes in government, liberty and slavery, commonly approach nearest to each other; and that, as you depart from the extremes, and mix a little of monarchy with liberty, the government becomes always the more free; and, on the other hand, when you mix a little of liberty with monarchy, the yoke becomes always the more grievous and intolerable. In a government, such as that of France, which is absolute, and where law, custom, and religion concur, all of them, to make the people fully satisfied with their condition, the monarch cannot entertain any *jealousy* against his subjects, and therefore is apt to indulge them in great *liberties*, both of speech and action. In a government altogether republican, such as that of Holland, where there is no magistrate so eminent as to give *jealousy* to the state, there is no danger in intrusting the magistrates with large discretionary powers; and though many advantages result from such powers, in preserving peace and order, yet they lay a considerable restraint on men's actions, and make every private citizen pay a great respect to the government. Thus it seems evident, that the two extremes of absolute monarchy and of a republic, approach near to each other in some material circumstances. In the *first*, the magistrate has no jealousy of the people; in the *second*, the people have none of the magistrate: which want of jealousy begets a mutual confidence and trust in both cases, and produces a species of liberty in monarchies, and of arbitrary power in republics.

To justify the other part of the foregoing observation, that, in every government, the means are most wide of each other, and that the mixtures of monarchy and liberty render the yoke either more grievous; I must take notice of a remark in Tacitus with regard to the Romans under the Emperors, that they neither could bear total slavery nor total liberty, *Nec totam servitutem, nec totam libertatem pati possunt.* This remark a celebrated poet has translated and applied to the English, in his lively description of Queen Elizabeth's policy and government.

> Et fit aimer son joug à l'Anglois indompté,
> Qui ne peut ni servir, ni vivre en liberté.

HENRIADE, liv. i.

According to these remarks, we are to consider the Roman government under the Emperors as a mixture of despotism and liberty, where the despotism prevailed; and the English government as a mixture of the same kind, where the liberty predominates. The consequences are conformable to the foregoing observation, and such as may be expected from those mixed forms of government, which beget a mutual watchfulness and jealousy. The Roman emperors were, many of them, the most frightful tyrants that ever disgraced human nature; and it is evident, that their cruelty was chiefly excited by their *jealousy*, and by their observing that all the great men of Rome bore with impatience the dominion of a family, which, but a little before, was nowise superior to their own. On the other hand, as the republican part of the government prevails in England, though with a great mixture of monarchy, it is obliged, for its own preservation, to maintain a watchful *jealousy* over the magistrates, to remove all discretionary powers, and to secure every one's life and fortune by general and inflexible laws. No action must be deemed a crime but what the law has plainly determined to be such: no crime must be imputed to a man but from a legal proof before his judges; and even these judges must be his fellow-subjects, who are obliged, by their own interest, to have a watchful eye over the encroachments and violence of the ministers. From these causes it proceeds, that there is as much liberty, and even perhaps licentiousness, in Great Britain, as there were formerly slavery and tyranny in Rome.

These principles account for the great liberty of the press in these kingdoms, beyond what is indulged in any other government. It is apprehended that arbitrary power would steal in upon us, were we not careful to prevent its progress, and were there not any easy method of conveying the alarm from one end of the kingdom to the other. The spirit of the people must frequently be roused, in order to curb the ambition of the court; and the dread of rousing this spirit must be employed to prevent that ambition. Nothing so effectual to this purpose as the liberty of the press; by which all the learning, wit, and genius of the nation, may be employed on the side of freedom, and every one be animated to its defence. As long, therefore, as the republican part of our government can maintain itself against the monarchical, it will naturally be careful to keep the press open, as of importance to its own preservation.[2]

---

[2] Since, therefore, the liberty of the press is so essential to the support of our mixed government, this sufficiently decides the second question, *Whether this liberty be advantageous or prejudicial,* there being nothing of greater importance in every state than the preservation of the ancient government, especially if it be a free one. But I would fain go a step further, and assert, that such a liberty is attended with so few inconveniences, that it may be claimed as the common right of mankind, and ought to be indulged them almost in every government except the ecclesiastical, to which, indeed, it would be fatal. We need not dread from this liberty any such ill consequences as followed from the

harangues of the popular demagogues of Athens and Tribunes of Rome. A man reads a book or pamphlet alone and coolly. There is none present from whom he can catch the passion by contagion. He is not hurried away by the force and energy of action. And should he be wrought up to never so seditious a humour, there is no violent resolution presented to him by which he can immediately vent his passion. The liberty of the press, therefore, however abused, can scarce ever excite popular tumults or rebellion. And as to those murmurs or secret discontents it may occasion, it is better they should get vent in words, that they may come to the knowledge of the magistrate before it be too late, in order to his providing a remedy against them. Mankind, it is true, have always a greater propension to believe what is said to the disadvantage of their governors than the contrary; but this inclination is inseparable from them whether they have liberty or not. A whisper may fly as quick, and be as pernicious as a pamphlet. Nay, it will be more pernicious, where men are not accustomed to think freely, or distinguish betwixt truth and falsehood.

It has also been found, as the experience of mankind increases, that the *people* are no such dangerous monsters as they have been represented, and that it is in every respect better to guide them like rational creatures than to lead or drive them like brute beasts. Before the United Provinces set the example, toleration was deemed incompatible with good government; and it was thought impossible that a number of religious sects could live together in harmony and peace, and have all of them an equal affection to their common country and to each other. *England* has set a like example of civil liberty; and though this liberty seems to occasion some small ferment at present, it has not as yet produced any pernicious effects; and it is to be hoped that men, being every day more accustomed to the free discussion of public affairs, will improve in their judgment of them, and be with greater difficulty seduced by every idle rumour and popular clamour.

It is a very comfortable reflection to the lovers of liberty, that this peculiar privilege of *Britain* is of a kind that cannot easily be wrested from us, and must last as long as our government remains in any degree free and independent. It is seldom that liberty of any kind is lost all at once. Slavery has so frightful an aspect to men accustomed to freedom, that it must steal in upon them by degrees, and must disguise itself in a thousand shapes in order to be received. But if the liberty of the press ever be lost, it must be lost at once. The general laws against sedition and libelling are at present as strong as they possibly can be made. Nothing can impose a further restraint but either the clapping an imprimatur upon the press, or the giving very large discretionary powers to the court to punish whatever displeases them. But these concessions would be such a barefaced violation of liberty, that they will probably be the last efforts of a despotic government. We may conclude that the liberty of *Britain* is gone for ever when these attempts shall succeed.

It must however be allowed, that the unbounded liberty of the press, though it be difficult, perhaps impossible, to propose a suitable remedy for it, is one of the evils attending those mixed forms of government.

THAT POLITICS MAY BE REDUCED TO A SCIENCE

It is a question with several, whether there be any essential difference between one form of government and another? and, whether every form may not become good or bad, according as it is well or ill administered?[3] Were it once admitted, that all governments are alike, and that the only difference consists in the character and conduct of the governors, most political disputes would be at an end, and all *Zeal* for one constitution above another must be esteemed mere bigotry and folly. But, though a friend to moderation, I cannot forbear condemning this sentiment, and should be sorry to think, that human affairs admit of no greater stability, than what they receive from the casual humours and characters of particular men.

It is true, those who maintain that the goodness of all government consists in the goodness of the administration, may cite many particular instances in history, where the very same government, in different hands, has varied suddenly into the two opposite extremes of good and bad. Compare the French government under Henry III and under Henry IV. Oppression, levity, artifice, on the part of the rulers; faction, sedition, treachery, rebellion, disloyalty on the part of the subjects: these compose the character of the former miserable era. But when the patriot and heroic prince, who succeeded, was once firmly seated on the throne, the government, the people, every thing, seemed to be totally changed; and all from the difference of the temper and conduct of these two sovereigns.[4] Instances of this kind may be multiplied, almost without number, from ancient as well as modern history, foreign as well as domestic.

---

[3] For forms of government let fools contest,
Whate'er is best administered is best.

--ESSAY ON MAN, Book 3.

[4] An equal difference of a contrary kind may be found in comparing the reigns of *Elizabeth* and *James*, at least with regard to foreign affairs.

But here it may be proper to make a distinction. All absolute governments must very much depend on the administration; and this is one of the great inconveniences attending that form of government. But a republican and free government would be an obvious absurdity, if the particular checks and controls, provided by the constitution had really no influence, and made it not the interest, even of bad men, to act for the public good. Such is the intention of these forms of government, and such is their real effect, where they are wisely constituted: as, on the other hand, they are the source of all disorder, and of the blackest crimes, where either skill or honesty has been wanting in their original frame and institution.

So great is the force of laws, and of particular forms of government, and so little dependence have they on the humours and tempers of men, that consequences almost as general and certain may sometimes be deduced from them, as any which the mathematical sciences afford us.

The constitution of the Roman republic gave the whole legislative power to the people, without allowing a negative voice either to the nobility or consuls. This unbounded power they possessed in a collective, not in a representative body. The consequences were: when the people, by success and conquest, had become very numerous, and had spread themselves to a great distance from the capital, the city tribes, though the most contemptible, carried almost every vote: they were, therefore, most cajoled by every one that affected popularity: they were supported in idleness by the general distribution of corn, and by particular bribes, which they received from almost every candidate: by this means, they became every day more licentious, and the Campus Martius was a perpetual scene of tumult and sedition: armed slaves were introduced among these rascally citizens, so that the whole government fell into anarchy; and the greatest happiness which the Romans could look for, was the despotic power of the Cæsars. Such are the effects of democracy without a representative.

A Nobility may possess the whole, or any part of the legislative power of a state, in two different ways. Either every nobleman shares the power as a part of the whole body, or the whole body enjoys the power as composed of parts, which have each a distinct power and authority. The Venetian aristocracy is an instance of the first kind of government; the Polish, of the second. In the Venetian government the whole body of nobility possesses the whole power, and no nobleman has any authority which he receives not from the whole. In the Polish government every nobleman, by means of his fiefs, has a distinct hereditary authority over his vassals, and the whole body has no authority but what it receives from the concurrence of its parts. The different operations and tendencies of these two species of government might be made apparent even *a priori*. A Venetian nobility is preferable to a Polish, let the humours and education of men be ever so much varied. A nobility, who possess their power in common, will preserve peace and order, both among themselves, and their subjects; and no member can have authority enough to control the laws for a moment. The nobles will preserve their authority over the people, but without any grievous tyranny, or any breach of private property; because such a tyrannical government promotes not the interests of the whole body, however it may that of some individuals. There will be a distinction of rank between the nobility and people, but this will be the only distinction in the state. The whole nobility will form one body, and the whole people another, without any of those private feuds and animosities, which spread ruin and desolation everywhere. It is easy to see the disadvantages of a Polish nobility in every one of these particulars.

It is possible so to constitute a free government, as that a single person, call him a doge, prince, or king, shall possess a large share of power, and shall form a proper balance or counterpoise to the other parts of the legislature. This chief magistrate may be either *elective* or *hereditary*, and though the former institution may, to a superficial view, appear the most advantageous; yet a more accurate inspection will discover in it greater inconveniences than in the latter, and such as are founded on causes and principles eternal and immutable. The filling of the throne, in such a government, is a point of too great and too general interest, not to divide the whole people into factions, whence a civil war, the greatest of ills, may be apprehended, almost with certainty, upon every vacancy. The prince elected must be either a *Foreigner* or a *Native*: the former will be ignorant of the people whom he is to govern; suspicious of his new subjects, and suspected by them; giving his confidence entirely to strangers, who will have no other care but of enriching themselves in the quickest manner, while their master's favour and authority are able to support them. A native will carry into the throne all his private animosities and friendships, and will never be viewed in his elevation without exciting the sentiment of envy in those who formerly considered him as their equal. Not to mention that a crown is too high a reward ever to be given to merit alone, and will always induce the candidates to employ force, or money, or intrigue, to procure the votes of the electors: so that such an election will give no better chance for superior merit in the prince, than if the state had trusted to birth alone for determining the sovereign.

It may, therefore, be pronounced as an universal axiom in politics, *That an hereditary prince, a nobility without vassals, and a people voting by their representatives, form the best* MONARCHY, ARISTOCRACY, *and* DEMOCRACY. But in order to prove more fully, that politics admit of general truths, which are invariable by the humour or education either of subject or sovereign, it may not be amiss to observe some other principles of this science, which may seem to deserve that character.

It may easily be observed, that though free governments have been commonly the most happy for those who partake of their freedom; yet are they the most ruinous and oppressive to their provinces: and this observation may, I believe, be fixed as a maxim of the kind we are here speaking of. When a monarch extends his dominions by conquest, he soon learns to consider his old and his new subjects as on the same footing; because, in reality, all his subjects are to him the same, except the few friends and favourites with whom he is personally acquainted. He does not, therefore, make any distinction between them in his *general* laws; and, at the same time, is careful to prevent all *particular* acts of oppression on the one as well as the other. But a free state necessarily makes a great distinction, and must always do so till men learn to love their neighbours as well as themselves. The conquerors, in such a government, are all legislators, and will be sure to contrive matters, by restrictions on trade, and by taxes, so as to draw some private, as well as public advantage from their conquests. Provincial governors have also a better chance, in a republic, to escape with their plunder, by means of bribery or intrigue; and their fellow-citizens, who find their own state to be enriched by the spoils of the subject provinces, will be the more inclined to tolerate such abuses. Not to mention, that it is a necessary precaution in a free state to change the governors frequently, which obliges these temporary tyrants to be more expeditious and rapacious, that they may accumulate sufficient wealth before they give place to their successors. What cruel tyrants were the Romans over the world during the time of their commonwealth! It is true, they had laws to prevent oppression in their provincial magistrates; but Cicero informs us, that the Romans could not better consult the interests of the provinces than by repealing these very laws. For, in that case, says he, our magistrates, having entire impunity, would plunder no more than would satisfy their own rapaciousness; whereas, at present, they must also satisfy that of their judges, and of all the great men in Rome, of whose protection they stand in need. Who can read of the cruelties and oppressions of Verres without horror and astonishment? And who is not touched with indignation to hear, that, after Cicero had exhausted on that abandoned criminal all the thunders of his eloquence, and had prevailed so far as to get him condemned to the utmost extent of the laws, yet that cruel tyrant lived peaceably to old age, in opulence and ease, and, thirty years afterwards, was put into the proscription by Mark Antony, on account of his exorbitant wealth, where he fell with Cicero himself, and all the most virtuous men of Rome? After the dissolution of the commonwealth, the Roman yoke became easier upon the provinces, as Tacitus informs us; and it may be observed, that many of the worst emperors, Domitian, for instance, were careful to prevent all oppression on the provinces. In Tiberius's time, Gaul was esteemed richer than Italy itself: nor do I find, during the whole time of the Roman monarchy, that the empire became less rich or populous in any of its provinces; though indeed its valour and military discipline were always upon the decline. The oppression and tyranny of the Carthaginians over their subject states in Africa went so far, as we learn from Polybius, that, not content with exacting the half of all the produce of the land, which of itself was a very high rent, they also loaded them with many other taxes. If we pass from ancient to modern times, we shall still find the observation to hold. The provinces of absolute monarchies are always better treated than those of free states. Compare the *Pais conquis* of France with Ireland, and you will be convinced of this truth; though this latter kingdom, being in a good measure peopled from England, possesses so many rights and privileges as should naturally make it challenge better treatment than that of a conquered province. Corsica is also an obvious instance to the same purpose.

There is an observation of Machiavel, with regard to the conquests of Alexander the Great, which, I think, may be regarded as one of those eternal political truths, which no time nor accidents can vary. It may seem strange, says that politician, that such sudden conquests, as those of Alexander, should be possessed so peaceably by his successors, and that the Persians, during all the confusions and civil wars among the Greeks, never made the smallest effort towards the recovery of their former independent government. To satisfy us concerning the cause of this remarkable event, we may consider, that a monarch may govern his subjects in two different ways. He may either follow the maxims of the Eastern princes, and stretch his authority so far as to leave no distinction of rank among his subjects, but what proceeds immediately from himself; no advantages of birth; no hereditary honours and possessions; and, in a word, no credit among the people, except from his commission alone. Or a monarch may exert his power after a milder manner, like other European princes; and leave other sources of honour, beside his smile and favour; birth, titles, possessions, valour, integrity, knowledge, or great and fortunate achievements. In the former species of government, after a conquest, it is impossible ever to shake off the yoke; since no one possesses, among the people, so much personal credit and authority as to begin such an enterprise: whereas, in the latter, the least misfortune, or discord among the victors, will encourage the vanquished to take arms, who have leaders ready to prompt and conduct them in every undertaking.[5]

---

[5] I have taken it for granted, according to the supposition of Machiavel, that the ancient Persians had no nobility; though there is reason to suspect, that the Florentine secretary, who seems to have been better acquainted with the Roman than the Greek authors, was mistaken in this particular. The more ancient Persians, whose manners are described by Xenophon, were a free people, and had nobility. Their ομοτιμοι were preserved even after the extending of their conquests and the consequent change of their government. Arrian mentions them in Darius's time, *De exped. Alex.* lib. ii. Historians also speak often of the persons in command as men of family. Tygranes, who was general of the Medes under Xerxes, was of the race of Achmænes, Heriod. lib. vii. cap. 62. Artachæus, who directed the cutting of the canal about Mount Athos, was of the same family. Id. cap. 117. Megabyzus was one of the seven eminent Persians who conspired against the Magi. His son, Zopyrus, was in the highest command under Darius, and delivered Babylon to him. His grandson, Megabyzus, commanded the army defeated at Marathon. His great-grandson, Zopyrus, was also eminent, and was banished Persia. Heriod. lib. iii. Thuc. lib. i. Rosaces, who commanded an army in Egypt under Artaxerxes, was also descended from one of the seven conspirators, Diod. Sic. lib. xvi. Agesilaus, in Xenophon. Hist. Græc. lib. iv. being desirous of making a marriage betwixt king Cotys his ally, and the daughter of Spithridates, a Persian of rank, who had deserted to him, first asks Cotys what family Spithridates is of. One of the most considerable in Persia, says Cotys. Ariæus, when offered the sovereignty by Clearchus and the ten thousand Greeks, refused it as of too low a rank, and said, that so many eminent Persians would never endure his rule. *Id. de exped.* lib. ii. Some of the families descended from the seven Persians above mentioned remained during Alexander's successors; and Mithridates, in Antiochus's time, is said by Polybius to be descended from one of them, lib. v. cap. 43. Artabazus was esteemed as Arrian says, εν τοις πρωτοις Περσων, lib.

Such is the reasoning of Machiavel, which seems solid and conclusive; though I wish he had not mixed falsehood with truth, in asserting that monarchies, governed according to Eastern policy, though more easily kept when once subdued, yet are the most difficult to subdue; since they cannot contain any powerful subject, whose discontent and faction may facilitate the enterprises of an enemy. For, besides, that such a tyrannical government enervates the courage of men, and renders them indifferent towards the fortunes of their sovereigns; besides this, I say, we find by experience, that even the temporary and delegated authority of the generals and magistrates, being always, in such governments, as absolute within its sphere as that of the prince himself, is able, with barbarians accustomed to a blind submission, to produce the most dangerous and fatal revolutions. So that in every respect, a gentle government is preferable, and gives the greatest security to the sovereign as well as to the subject.

Legislators, therefore, ought not to trust the future government of a state entirely to chance, but ought to provide a system of laws to regulate the administration of public affairs to the latest posterity. Effects will always correspond to causes; and wise regulations, in any commonwealth, are the most valuable legacy that can be left to future ages. In the smallest court or office, the stated forms and methods by which business must be conducted, are found to be a considerable check on the natural depravity of mankind. Why should not the case be the same in

---

iii. And when Alexander married in one day 80 of his captains to Persian women, his intention plainly was to ally the Macedonians with the most eminent Persian families. Id. lib. vii. Diodorus Siculus says, they were of the most noble birth in Persia, lib. xvii. The government of Persia was despotic, and conducted in many respects after the Eastern manner, but was not carried so far as to extirpate all nobility, and confound all ranks and orders. It left men who were still great, by themselves and their family, independent of their office and commission. And the reason why the Macedonians kept so easily dominion over them, was owing to other causes easy to be found in the historians, though it must be owned that Machiavel's reasoning is, in itself, just, however doubtful its application to the present case.

public affairs? Can we ascribe the stability and wisdom of the Venetian government, through so many ages, to any thing but the form of government? And is it not easy to point out those defects in the original constitution, which produced the tumultuous governments of Athens and Rome, and ended at last in the ruin of these two famous republics? And so little dependence has this affair on the humours and education of particular men, that one part of the same republic may be wisely conducted, and another weakly, by the very same men, merely on account of the differences of the forms and institutions by which these parts are regulated. Historians inform us that this was actually the case with Genoa. For while the state was always full of sedition, and tumult, and disorder, the bank of St. George, which had become a considerable part of the people, was conducted, for several ages, with the utmost integrity and wisdom.

The ages of greatest public spirit are not always most eminent for private virtue. Good laws may beget order and moderation in the government, where the manners and customs have instilled little humanity or justice into the tempers of men. The most illustrious period of the Roman history, considered in a political view, is that between the beginning of the first and end of the last Punic war; the due balance between the nobility and people being then fixed by the contests of the tribunes, and not being yet lost by the extent of conquests. Yet at this very time, the horrid practice of poisoning was so common, that, during part of the season, a *Prætor* punished capitally for this crime above three thousand persons in a part of Italy; and found informations of this nature still multiplying upon him. There is a similar, or rather a worse instance, in the more early times of the commonwealth; so depraved in private life were that people, whom in their histories we so much admire. I doubt not but they were really more virtuous during the time of the two *Triumvirates*, when they were tearing their common country to pieces, and spreading slaughter and desolation over the face of the earth, merely for the choice of tyrants.

Here, then, is a sufficient inducement to maintain, with the utmost zeal, in every free state, those forms and institutions by which liberty is secured, the public good consulted, and the avarice or ambition of particular men restrained and punished. Nothing does more honour to human nature, than to see it susceptible of so noble a passion; as nothing can be a greater indication of meanness of heart in any man than to see him destitute of it. A man who loves only himself, without regard to friendship and desert, merits the severest blame; and a man, who is only susceptible of friendship, without public spirit, or a regard to the community, is deficient in the most material part of virtue.

But this is a subject which needs not be longer insisted on at present. There are enow of zealots on both sides, who kindle up the passions of their partisans, and, under pretence of public good, pursue the interests and ends of their particular faction. For my part, I shall always be more fond of promoting moderation than zeal; though perhaps the surest way of producing moderation in every party is to increase our zeal for the public. Let us therefore try, if it be possible, from the foregoing doctrine, to draw a lesson of moderation with regard to the parties into which our country is at present divided; at the same time, that we allow not this moderation to abate the industry and passion, with which every individual is bound to pursue the good of his country.

Those who either attack or defend a minister in such a government as ours, where the utmost liberty is allowed, always carry matters to an extreme, and exaggerate his merit or demerit with regard to the public. His enemies are sure to charge him with the greatest enormities, both in domestic and foreign management; and there is no meanness or crime, of which, in their account, he is not capable. Unnecessary wars, scandalous treaties, profusion of public treasure, oppressive taxes, every kind of maladministration is ascribed to him. To aggravate the charge, his pernicious conduct, it is said, will extend its baneful influence even to posterity, by undermining the best constitution in the world, and disordering that wise system of laws, institutions, and customs, by which our ancestors, during so many centuries, have been so happily governed. He is not only a wicked minister in himself, but has removed every security provided against wicked ministers for the future.

On the other hand, the partisans of the minister make his panegyric run as high as the accusation against him, and celebrate his wise, steady, and moderate conduct in every part of his administration. The honour and interest of the nation supported abroad, public credit maintained at home, persecution restrained, faction subdued; the merit of all these blessings is ascribed solely to the minister. At the same time, he crowns all his other merits by a religious care of the best constitution in the world, which he has preserved in all its parts, and has transmitted entire, to be the happiness and security of the latest posterity.

When this accusation and panegyric are received by the partisans of each party, no wonder they beget an extraordinary ferment on both sides, and fill the nation with violent animosities. But I would fain persuade these party zealots, that there is a flat contradiction both in the accusation and panegyric, and that it were impossible for either of them to run so high, were it not for this contradiction. If our constitution be really *that noble fabric, the pride of Britain, the envy of our neighbours, raised by the labour of so many centuries, repaired at the expense of so many millions, and cemented by such a profusion of blood*;[6] I say, if our constitution does in any degree deserve these eulogies, it would never have suffered a wicked and weak minister to govern triumphantly for a course of twenty years, when opposed by the greatest geniuses in the nation, who exercised the utmost liberty of tongue and pen, in parliament, and in their frequent appeals to the people. But, if the minister be wicked and weak, to the degree so strenuously insisted on, the constitution must be faulty in its original principles, and he cannot consistently be charged with undermining the best form of government in the world. A constitution is only so far good, as it provides a remedy against

---

[6] Dissertation on Parties, Letter X.

maladministration; and if the British, when in its greatest vigour, and repaired by two such remarkable events as the *Revolution* and *Accession*, by which our ancient royal family was sacrificed to it; if our constitution, I say, with so great advantages, does not, in fact, provide any such remedy, we are rather beholden to any minister who undermines it, and affords us an opportunity of erecting a better in its place.

I would employ the same topics to moderate the zeal of those who defend the minister. *Is our constitution so excellent?* Then a change of ministry can be no such dreadful event; since it is essential to such a constitution, in every ministry, both to preserve itself from violation, and to prevent all enormities in the administration. *Is our constitution very bad?* Then so extraordinary a jealousy and apprehension, on account of changes, is ill placed; and a man should no more be anxious in this case, than a husband, who had married a woman from the stews, should be watchful to prevent her infidelity. Public affairs, in such a government, must necessarily go to confusion, by whatever hands they are conducted; and the zeal of *patriots* is in that case much less requisite than the patience and submission of *philosophers*. The virtue and good intention of Cato and Brutus are highly laudable; but to what purpose did their zeal serve? Only to hasten the fatal period of the Roman government, and render its convulsions and dying agonies more violent and painful.

I would not be understood to mean, that public affairs deserve no care and attention at all. Would men be moderate and consistent, their claims might be admitted; at least might be examined. The *country party* might still assert, that our constitution, though excellent, will admit of maladministration to a certain degree; and therefore, if the minister be bad, it is proper to oppose him with a *suitable* degree of zeal. And, on the other hand, the *court party* may be allowed, upon the supposition that the minister were good, to defend, and with some zeal too, his administration. I would only persuade men not to contend, as if they were fighting *pro aris et focis*, and change a good constitution into a bad one, by the violence of their factions.

I have not here considered any thing that is personal in the present controversy. In the best civil constitutions, where every man is restrained by the most rigid laws, it is easy to discover either the good or bad intentions of a minister, and to judge whether his personal character deserve love or hatred. But such questions are of little importance to the public, and lay those who employ their pens upon them, under a just suspicion either of malevolence or of flattery.[7]

---

[7] *What our author's opinion was of the famous minister here pointed at, may be learned from that Essay, printed in the former edition, under the title of* 'A Character of Sir Robert Walpole.' *It was as follows:*—There never was a man whose actions and character have been more earnestly and openly canvassed than those of the present minister, who, having governed a learned and free nation for so long a time, amidst such mighty opposition, may make a large library of what has been wrote for and against him, and is the subject of above half the paper that has been blotted in the nation within these twenty years. I wish, for the honour of our country, that any one character of him had been drawn with such *judgment* and *impartiality* as to have some credit with posterity, and to show that our liberty has, once at least, employed to good purpose. I am only afraid of failing in the former quality of judgment; but if it should be so, it is but one page more thrown away, after an hundred thousand upon the same subject, that have perished and become useless. In the mean time, I shall flatter myself with the pleasing imagination, that the following character will be adopted by future historians.

Sir Robert Walpole, Prime Minister of *Great Britain*, is a man of ability, not a genius; good-natured, not virtuous; constant, not magnanimous; moderate, not equitable.[Moderate in the exercise of power, not equitable in engrossing it.] His virtues, in some instances, are free from the alloy of those vices which usually accompany such virtues; he is a generous friend, without being a bitter enemy. His vices, in other instances, are not compensated by those virtues which are nearly allied to them: his want of enterprise is not attended with frugality. The private character of the man is better than the public: his virtues more than his vices: his fortune greater than his fame. With many good qualities, he has incurred the public hatred: with good capacity, he has not escaped ridicule. He would have been esteemed more worthy of his high station, had he never possessed it; and is better qualified for the second than for the first place in any government; his ministry has been more advantageous to his family than to the public, better for this age than for posterity; and more pernicious by bad precedents than by real grievances. During his time trade has flourished, liberty declined, and learning gone to ruin. As I am a man, I love him; as I am a scholar, I hate him; as I am a *Briton*,

I calmly wish his fall. And were I a member of either House, I would give my vote for removing him from St James's; but should be glad to see him retire to *Houghton-Hall*, to pass the remainder of his days in ease and pleasure.

The author is pleased to find, that after animosities are laid, and calumny has ceased, the whole nation almost have returned to the same moderate sentiments with regard to this great man, if they are not rather become more favourable to him, by a very natural transition, from one extreme to another. The author would not oppose these humane sentiments towards the dead; though he cannot forbear observing, that the not paying more of our public debts was, as hinted in this character, a great, and the only great, error in that long administration.

OF THE FIRST PRINCIPLES OF GOVERNMENT

Nothing appears more surprising to those who consider human affairs with a philosophical eye, than the easiness with which the many are governed by the few; and the implicit submission, with which men resign their own sentiments and passions to those of their rulers. When we enquire by what means this wonder is effected, we shall find, that, as Force is always on the side of the governed, the governors have nothing to support them but opinion. It is, therefore, on opinion only that government is founded; and this maxim extends to the most despotic and most military governments, as well as to the most free and most popular. The soldan of Egypt, or the emperor of Rome, might drive his harmless subjects, like brute beasts, against their sentiments and inclination. But he must, at least, have led his *mamalukes* or *prætorian bands*, like men, by their opinion.

Opinion is of two kinds, to wit, opinion of interest, and opinion of right. By opinion of INTEREST, I chiefly understand the sense of the general advantage which is reaped from government; together with the persuasion, that the particular government which is established is equally advantageous with any other that could easily be settled. When this opinion prevails among the generality of a state, or among those who have the force in their hands, it gives great security to any government.

Right is of two kinds; right to Power, and right to Property. What prevalence opinion of the first kind has over mankind, may easily be understood, by observing the attachment which all nations have to their ancient government, and even to those names which have had the sanction of antiquity. Antiquity always begets the opinion of right; and whatever disadvantageous sentiments we may entertain of mankind, they are always found to be prodigal both of blood and treasure in the maintenance of public justice.[8] There is, indeed, no particular in which, at first

---

[8] This passion we may denominate enthusiasm, or we may give it what appellation we please; but a politician who should overlook its influence on human affairs, would prove himself to have but a very limited understanding.

sight, there may appear a greater contradiction in the frame of the human mind than the present. When men act in a faction, they are apt, without shame or remorse, to neglect all the ties of honour and morality, in order to serve their party; and yet, when a faction is formed upon a point of right or principle, there is no occasion where men discover a greater obstinacy, and a more determined sense of justice and equity. The same social disposition of mankind is the cause of these contradictory appearances.

It is sufficiently understood, that the opinion of right to property is of moment in all matters of government. A noted author has made property the foundation of all government; and most of our political writers seem inclined to follow him in that particular. This is carrying the matter too far; but still it must be owned, that the opinion of right to property has a great influence in this subject.

Upon these three opinions, therefore, of public *interest*, of *right to power*, and of *right to property*, are all governments founded, and all authority of the few over the many. There are indeed other principles which add force to these, and determine, limit, or alter their operation; such as *self-interest*, *fear*, and *affection*. But still we may assert, that these other principles can have no influence alone, but suppose the antecedent influence of those opinions above mentioned. They are, therefore, to be esteemed the secondary, not the original, principles of government.

For, *first*, as to *self-interest*, by which I mean the expectation of particular rewards, distinct from the general protection which we receive from government, it is evident that the magistrate's authority must be antecedently established, at least be hoped for, in order to produce this expectation. The prospect of reward may augment his authority with regard to some particular persons, but can never give birth to it, with regard to the public. Men naturally look for the greatest favours from their friends and acquaintance; and therefore, the hopes of any considerable number of the state would never centre in any particular set of men, if these men had no other title to magistracy, and had no separate influence over the opinions of mankind. The same observation may be extended to the other two principles of *fear* and *affection*. No man would have any reason to *fear* the fury of a tyrant, if he had no authority over any but from fear; since, as a single man, his bodily force can reach but a small way, and all the further power he possesses must be founded either on our own opinion, or on the presumed opinion of others. And though *affection* to wisdom and virtue in a *sovereign* extends very far, and has great influence, yet he must antecedently be supposed invested with a public character, otherwise the public esteem will serve him in no stead, nor will his virtue have any influence beyond a narrow sphere.

A government may endure for several ages, though the balance of power and the balance of property do not coincide. This chiefly happens where any rank or order of the state has acquired a large share in the property; but, from the original constitution of the government, has no share in the power. Under what pretence would any individual of that order assume authority in public affairs? As men are commonly much attached to their ancient government, it is not to be expected, that the public would ever favour such usurpations. But where the original constitution allows any share of power, though small, to an order of men who possess a large share of property, it is easy for them gradually to stretch their authority, and bring the balance of power to coincide with that of property. This has been the case with the House of Commons in England.

Most writers that have treated of the British government, have supposed, that, as the Lower House represents all the Commons of Great Britain, its weight in the scale is proportioned to the property and power of all whom it represents. But this principle must not be received as absolutely true. For though the people are apt to attach themselves more to the House of Commons than to any other member of the constitution, that House being chosen by them as their representatives, and as the public guardians of their liberty; yet are there instances where the House, even when in opposition to the crown, has not been followed by the people, as we may particularly observe of the *Tory* House of Commons in the reign of King William. Were the members obliged to receive instructions from their constituents, like the Dutch deputies, this would entirely alter the case; and if such immense power and riches, as those of all the Commons of Great Britain, were brought into the scale, it is not easy to conceive, that the crown could either influence that multitude of people, or withstand the balance of property. It is true, the crown has great influence over the collective body in the elections of members; but were this influence, which at present is only exerted once in seven years, to be employed in bringing over the people to every vote, it would soon be wasted, and no skill, popularity, or revenue, could support it. I must, therefore, be of opinion, that an alteration in this particular would introduce a total alteration in our government, and would soon reduce it to a pure republic; and, perhaps, to a republic of no inconvenient form. For though the people, collected in a body like the Roman tribes, be quite unfit for government, yet, when dispersed in small bodies, they are most susceptible both of reason and order; the force of popular currents and tides is in a great measure broken; and the public interests may be pursued with some method and constancy. But it is needless to reason any further concerning a form of government, which is never likely to have place in Great Britain, and which seems not to be the aim of any party amongst us. Let us cherish and improve our ancient government as much as possible, without encouraging a passion for such dangerous novelties.[9]

---

[9] I shall conclude this subject with observing, that the present political controversy with regard to *instructions*, is a very frivolous one, and can never be brought to any decision, as it is managed by both parties. The country party do not pretend that a member is absolutely bound to follow instructions as an ambassador or general is confined by his orders, and that his vote is not to be received in the House, but so far as it is conformable to them. The court party, again, do not pretend that the sentiments of the people ought to have no weight with every member; much less that he ought to despise the sentiments of those whom he represents, and with whom he is more particularly connected. And if their sentiments be of weight, why ought they not to express

these sentiments? The question then is only concerning the degrees of weight which ought to be placed on instructions. But such is the nature of language, that it is impossible for it to express distinctly these different degrees; and if men will carry on a controversy on this head, it may well happen that they differ in the language, and yet agree in their sentiments; or differ in their sentiments, and yet agree in their language. Besides, how is it possible to fix these degrees, considering the variety of affairs that come before the House, and the variety of places which members represent? Ought the instructions of *Totness* to have the same weight as those of London? or instructions with regard to the *Convention* which respected foreign politics to have the same weight as those with regard to the *Excise*, which respected only our domestic affairs?

OF THE ORIGIN OF GOVERNMENT

Man, born in a family, is compelled to maintain society from necessity, from natural inclination, and from habit. The same creature, in his further progress, is engaged to establish political society, in order to administer justice, without which there can be no peace among them, nor safety, nor mutual intercourse. We are, therefore, to look upon all the vast apparatus of our government, as having ultimately no other object or purpose but the distribution of justice, or, in other words, the support of the twelve judges. Kings and parliaments, fleets and armies, officers of the court and revenue, ambassadors, ministers, and privy counsellors, are all subordinate in their end to this part of administration. Even the clergy, as their duty leads them to inculcate morality, may justly be thought, so far as regards this world, to have no other useful object of their institution.

All men are sensible of the necessity of justice to maintain peace and order; and all men are sensible of the necessity of peace and order for the maintenance of society. Yet, notwithstanding this strong and obvious necessity, such is the frailty or perverseness of our nature! it is impossible to keep men faithfully and unerringly in the paths of justice. Some extraordinary circumstances may happen, in which a man finds his interests to be more promoted by fraud or rapine, than hurt by the breach which his injustice makes in the social union. But much more frequently he is seduced from his great and important, but distant interests, by the allurement of present, though often very frivolous temptations. This great weakness is incurable in human nature.

Men must, therefore, endeavour to palliate what they cannot cure. They must institute some persons under the appellation of magistrates, whose peculiar office it is to point out the decrees of equity, to punish transgressors, to correct fraud and violence, and to oblige men, however reluctant, to consult their own real and permanent interests. In a word, obedience is a new duty which must be invented to support that of justice, and the ties of equity must be corroborated by those of allegiance.

But still, viewing matters in an abstract light, it may be thought that nothing is gained by this alliance, and that the factitious duty of obedience, from its very nature, lays as feeble a hold of the human mind, as the primitive and natural duty of justice. Peculiar interests and present temptations may overcome the one as well as the other. They are equally exposed to the same inconvenience; and the man who is inclined to be a bad neighbour, must be led by the same motives, well or ill understood, to be a bad citizen or subject. Not to mention, that the magistrate himself may often be negligent, or partial, or unjust in his administration.

Experience, however, proves that there is a great difference between the cases. Order in society, we find, is much better maintained by means of government; and our duty to the magistrate is more strictly guarded by the principles of human nature, than our duty to our fellow-citizens. The love of dominion, is so strong in the breast of man, that many not only submit to, but court all the dangers, and fatigues, and cares of government; and men, once raised to that station, though often led astray by private passions, find, in ordinary cases, a visible interest in the impartial administration of justice. The persons who first attain this distinction, by the consent, tacit or express, of the people, must be endowed with superior personal qualities of valour, force, integrity, or prudence, which command respect and confidence; and, after government is established, a regard to birth, rank, and station, has a mighty influence over men, and enforces the decrees of the magistrate. The prince or leader exclaims against every disorder which disturbs his society. He summons all his partisans and all men of probity to aid him in correcting and redressing it, and he is readily followed by all indifferent persons in the execution of his office. He soon acquires the power of rewarding these services; and in the progress of society, he establishes subordinate ministers, and often a military force, who find an immediate and a visible interest in supporting his authority. Habit soon consolidates what other principles of human nature had imperfectly founded; and men, once accustomed to obedience, never think of departing from that path, in which they and their ancestors have constantly trod, and to which they are confined by so many urgent and visible motives.

But though this progress of human affairs may appear certain and inevitable, and though the support which allegiance brings to justice be founded on obvious principles of human nature, it cannot be expected that men should beforehand be able to discover them, or foresee their operation. Government commences more casually and more imperfectly. It is probable, that the first ascendent of one man over multitudes began during a state of war; where the superiority of courage and of genius discovers itself most visibly, where unanimity and concert are most requisite, and where the pernicious effects of disorder are most sensibly felt. The long continuance of that state, an incident common among savage tribes, inured the people to submission; and if the chieftain possessed as much equity as prudence and valour, he became, even during peace, the arbiter of all differences, and could gradually, by a mixture of force and consent, establish his authority. The benefit sensibly felt from his influence, made it be cherished by the people, at least by the peaceable and well disposed among them; and if his son enjoyed the same good qualities, government advanced the sooner to maturity and perfection; but was still in a feeble state, till the further progress of improvement procured the magistrate a revenue, and enabled him to bestow rewards on the several instruments of his administration, and to inflict punishments on the refractory and disobedient. Before that period, each exertion of his influence must have been particular, and founded on the peculiar circumstances of the case. After it, submission was no longer a matter of choice in the bulk of the community, but was rigorously exacted by the authority of the supreme magistrate.

In all governments, there is a perpetual intestine struggle, open or secret, between Authority and Liberty, and neither of them can ever absolutely prevail in the contest. A great sacrifice of liberty must necessarily be made in every government; yet even the authority, which confines liberty, can never, and perhaps ought never, in any constitution, to become quite entire and uncontrollable. The sultan is master of the life and fortune of any individual; but will not be permitted to impose new taxes on his subjects: a French monarch can impose taxes at pleasure; but would find it dangerous to attempt the lives and fortunes of individuals. Religion also, in most countries, is commonly found to be a very intractable principle; and other principles or prejudices frequently resist all the authority of the civil magistrate; whose power, being founded on opinion, can never subvert other opinions equally rooted with that of his title to dominion. The government, which, in common appellation, receives the appellation of free, is that which admits of a partition of power among several members, whose united authority is no less, or is commonly greater, than that of any monarch; but who, in the usual course of administration, must act by general and equal laws, that are previously known to all the members, and to all their subjects. In this sense, it must be owned, that liberty is the perfection of civil society; but still authority must be acknowledged essential to its very existence: and in those contests which so often take place between the one and the other, the latter may, on that account, challenge the preference. Unless perhaps one may say (and it may be said with some reason) that a circumstance, which is essential to the existence of civil society, must always support itself, and needs be guarded with less jealousy, than one that contributes only to its perfection, which the indolence of men is so apt to neglect, or their ignorance to overlook.

OF THE INDEPENDENCY OF PARLIAMENT[10]

[10] I have frequently observed, in comparing the conduct of the *court* and *country* party, that the former are commonly less assuming and dogmatical in conversation, more apt to make concessions, and though not, perhaps, more susceptible of conviction, yet more able to bear contradiction than the latter, who are apt to fly out upon any opposition, and to regard one as a mercenary, designing fellow, if he argues with any coolness and impartiality, or makes any concessions to their adversaries. This is a fact, which, I believe, every one may have observed who has been much in companies where political questions have been discussed; though, were one to ask the reason of this difference, every party would be apt to assign a different reason. Gentlemen in the *opposition* will ascribe it to the very nature of their party, which, being founded on public spirit, and a zeal for the constitution, cannot easily endure such doctrines as are of pernicious consequence to liberty. The courtiers, on the other hand, will be apt to put us in mind of the clown mentioned by Lord Shaftesbury. 'A clown,' says that excellent author, 'once took a fancy to hear the *Latin* disputes of doctors at an university. He was asked what pleasure he could take in viewing such combatants, when he could never know so much as which of the parties had the better.'—'*For that matter,*' replied the clown, '*I a'n't such a fool neither, but I can see who's the first that puts t'other into a passion.*' Nature herself dictated this lesson to the clown, that he who had the better of the argument would be easy and well humoured: but he who was unable to support his cause by reason would naturally lose his temper, and grow violent.

To which of these reasons will we adhere? To neither of them, in my opinion, unless we have a mind to enlist ourselves and become zealots in either party. I believe I can assign the reason of this different conduct of the two parties, without offending either. The country party are plainly most popular at present, and perhaps have been so in most administrations so that, being accustomed to prevail in company, they cannot endure to hear their opinions controverted, but are so confident on the public favour, as if they were supported in all their sentiments by the most infallible demonstration. The courtiers, on the other hand, are Commonly run down by your popular talkers, that if you speak to them with any moderation, or make them the smallest concessions, they think themselves extremely obliged to you, and are apt to return the favour by a like moderation and facility on their part. To be furious and passionate, they know, would only gain them the character of shameless mercenaries, not that of zealous patriots, which is the character that such a warm behaviour is apt to acquire to the other party.

In all controversies, we find, without regarding the truth or falsehood on either side, that those who defend the established and popular opinions are always most dogmatical and imperious in their style: while their adversaries affect almost extraordinary gentleness and moderation, in order to soften, as

Political writers have established it as a maxim, that, in contriving any system of government, and fixing the several checks and controls of the constitution, every man ought to be supposed a *knave*, and to have no other end, in all his actions, than private interest. By this interest we must govern him, and, by means of it, make him, notwithstanding his insatiable avarice and ambition, cooperate to public good. Without this, say they, we

---

much as possible, any prejudices that may be Against them. Consider the behaviour of our *Freethinkers* of all denominations, whether they be such as decry all revelation, or only oppose the exorbitant power of the clergy, Collins, Tindal, Foster, Hoadley. Compare their moderation and good manners with the furious zeal and scurrility of their adversaries, and you will be convinced of the truth of my observation. A like difference may be observed in the conduct of those French writers, who maintained the controversy with regard to ancient and modern learning. Boileau, Monsieur and Madame Dacier, l'Abbé de Bos, who defended the party of the ancients, mixed their reasonings with satire and invective, while Fontenelle, la Motte, Charpentier, and even Perrault, never transgressed the bounds of moderation and good breeding, though provoked by the most injurious treatment of their adversaries.

I must however observe, that this remark with regard to the seeming moderation of the *court* party, is entirely confined to conversation, and to gentlemen who have been engaged by interest or inclination in that party. For as to the court writers, being commonly hired scribblers, they are altogether as scurrilous as the mercenaries of the other party: nor has the *Gazetteer* any advantage, in this respect, above common sense. A man of education will, in any party, discover himself to be such by his goodbreeding and decency, as a scoundrel will always betray the opposite qualities. *The false accusers accused,* &c. is very scurrilous, though that side of the question, being least popular, should be defended with most moderation. When L—d B—e, L—d M—t, Mr. L—n, take the pen in hand, though they write with warmth, they presume not upon their popularity so far as to transgress the bounds of decency.

I am led into this train of reflection by considering some papers wrote upon that grand topic of *court influence and parliamentary dependence,* where, in my humble opinion, the country party show too rigid an inflexibility, and too great a jealousy of making concessions to their adversaries. Their reasonings lose their force by being carried too far and the popularity of their opinions has seduced them to neglect in some measure their justness and solidity. The following reasoning will, I hope, serve to justify me in this opinion.

shall in vain boast of the advantages of any constitution, and shall find, in the end, that we have no security for our liberties or possessions, except the good-will of our rulers; that is, we shall have no security at all.

It is, therefore, a just *political* maxim, *that every man must be supposed a knave*; though, at the same time, it appears somewhat strange, that a maxim should be true in *politics* which is false in *fact*. But to satisfy us on this head, we may consider, that men are generally more honest in their private than in their public capacity, and will go greater lengths to serve a party, than when their own private interest is alone concerned. Honour is a great check upon mankind: but where a considerable body of men act together, this check is in a great measure removed, since a man is sure to be approved of by his own party, for what promotes the common interest; and he soon learns to despise the clamours of adversaries. To which we may add, that every court or senate is determined by the greater number of voices; so that, if self-interest influences only the majority (as it will always do), the whole senate follows the allurements of this separate interest, and acts as if it contained not one member who had any regard to public interest and liberty.

When there offers, therefore, to our censure and examination, any plan of government, real or imaginary, where the power is distributed among several courts, and several orders of men, we should always consider the separate interest of each court, and each order; and if we find that, by the skilful division of power, this interest must necessarily, in its operation, concur with the public, we may pronounce that government to be wise and happy. If, on the contrary, separate interest be not checked, and be not directed to the public, we ought to look for nothing but faction, disorder, and tyranny from such a government. In this opinion I am justified by experience, as well as by the authority of all philosophers and politicians, both ancient and modern.

How much, therefore, would it have surprised such a genius as Cicero or Tacitus, to have been told, that in a future age there should arise a very regular system of *mixed* government, where the authority was so distributed, that one rank, whenever it pleased, might swallow up all the rest, and engross the whole power of the constitution! Such a government, they would say, will not be a mixed government. For so great is the natural ambition of men, that they are never satisfied with power; and if one order of men, by pursuing its own interest, can usurp upon every other order, it will certainly do so, and render itself, as far as possible, absolute and uncontrollable.

But, in this opinion, experience shows they would have been mistaken. For this is actually the case with the British constitution. The share of power allotted by our constitution to the House of Commons, is so great, that it absolutely commands all the other parts of the government. The king's legislative power is plainly no proper check to it. For though the king has a negative in framing laws, yet this, in fact, is esteemed of so little moment, that whatever is voted by the two Houses, is always sure to pass into a law, and the royal assent is little better than a form. The principal weight of the crown lies in the executive; power. But, besides that the executive power in every government is altogether subordinate to the legislative; besides this, I say, the exercise of this power requires an immense expense, and the Commons have assumed to themselves the sole right of granting money. How easy, therefore, would it be for that house to wrest from the crown all these powers, one after another, by making every grant conditional, and choosing their time so well, that their refusal of supply should only distress the government, without giving foreign powers any advantage over us! Did the House of Commons depend in the same manner upon the king, and had none of the members any property but from his gift, would not he command all their resolutions, and be from that moment absolute? As to the House of Lords, they are a very powerful support to the crown, so long as they are, in their turn, supported by it; but both experience and reason show, that they have no force or authority sufficient to maintain themselves alone, without such support.

How, therefore, shall we solve this paradox? And by what means is this member of our constitution confined within the proper limits, since, from our very constitution, it must necessarily have as much power as it demands, and can only be confined by itself? How is this consistent with our experience of human nature? I answer, that the interest of the body is here restrained by that of the individuals, and that the House of Commons stretches not its power, because such an usurpation would be contrary to the interest of the majority of its members. The crown has so many offices at its disposal, that, when assisted by the honest and disinterested part of the House, it will always command the resolutions of the whole, so far, at least, as to preserve the ancient constitution from danger. We may, therefore, give to this influence what name we please; we may call it by the invidious appellations of *corruption* and *dependence*; but some degree and some kind of it are inseparable from the very nature of the constitution, and necessary to the preservation of our mixed government.

Instead, then, of asserting absolutely, that the dependence of parliament, in every degree, is an infringement of British liberty, the country party should have made some concessions to their adversaries, and have only examined what was the proper degree of this dependence, beyond which it became dangerous to liberty. But such a moderation is not to be expected in party men of any kind. After a concession of this nature, all declamation must be abandoned; and a calm inquiry into the proper degree of court influence and parliamentary dependence would have been expected by the readers. And though the advantage, in such a controversy, might possibly remain to the *country party*, yet the victory would not be so complete as they wish for, nor would a true patriot have given an entire loose to his zeal, for fear of running matters into a contrary extreme, by diminishing too [11] far

---

[11] By that *influence of the crown*, which I would justify, I mean only that which arises from the offices and honours that are at the disposal of the crown. As to private *bribery*, it may be considered in the same light as the practice of employing spies, which is scarcely justifiable in a good minister, and is

the influence of the crown. It was, therefore, thought best to deny that this extreme could ever be dangerous to the constitution, or that the crown could ever have too little influence over members of parliament.

All questions concerning the proper medium between extremes are difficult to be decided; both because it is not easy to find *words* proper to fix this medium, and because the good and ill, in such cases, run so gradually into each other, as even to render our *sentiments* doubtful and uncertain. But there is a peculiar difficulty in the present case, which would embarrass the most knowing and most impartial examiner. The power of the crown is always lodged in a single person, either king or minister; and as this person may have either a greater or less degree of ambition, capacity, courage, popularity, or fortune, the power, which is too great in one hand, may become too little in another. In pure republics, where the authority is distributed among several assemblies or senates, the checks and controls are more regular in their operation; because the members of such numerous assemblies may be presumed to be always nearly equal in capacity and virtue; and it is only their number, riches, or authority, which enter into consideration. But a limited monarchy admits not of any such stability; nor is it possible to assign to the crown such a determinate degree of power, as will, in every hand, form a proper counterbalance to the other parts of the constitution. This is an unavoidable disadvantage, among the many advantages attending that species of government.

---

infamous in a bad one; but to be a spy, or to be corrupted, is always infamous under all ministers, and is to be regarded as a shameless prostitution. Polybius justly esteems the pecuniary influence of the senate and censors to be one of the regular and constitutional weights which preserved the balance of the Roman government.—Lib. vi. cap. 15.

WHETHER THE BRITISH GOVERNMENT INCLINES MORE TO ABSOLUTE MONARCHY OR TO A REPUBLIC

It affords a violent prejudice against almost every science, that no prudent man, however sure of his principles, dares prophesy concerning any event, or foretell the remote consequences of things. A physician will not venture to pronounce concerning the condition of his patient a fortnight or a month after: and still less dares a politician foretell the situation of public affairs a few years hence. Harrington thought himself so sure of his general principle, *that the balance of power depends on that of property*, that he ventured to pronounce it impossible ever to reestablish monarchy in England: but his book was scarcely published when the king was restored; and we see that monarchy has ever since subsisted upon the same footing as before. Notwithstanding this unlucky example, I will venture to examine an important question, to wit, *Whether the British Government inclines more to absolute monarchy or to a republic; and in which of these two species of government it will most probably terminate?* As there seems not to be any great danger of a sudden revolution either way, I shall at least escape the shame attending my temerity, if I should be found to have been mistaken.

Those who assert that the balance of our government inclines towards absolute monarchy, may support their opinion by the following reasons: That property has a great influence on power cannot possibly be denied; but yet the general maxim, *that the balance of the one depends on the balance of the other*, must be received with several limitations. It is evident, that much less property in a single hand will be able to counterbalance a greater property in several; not only because it is difficult to make many persons combine in the same views and measures, but because property, when united, causes much greater dependence than the same property when dispersed. A hundred persons of £1,000 a year apiece, can consume all their income, and nobody shall ever be the better for them, except their servants and tradesmen, who justly regard their profits as the product of their own labour. But a man possessed of £100,000 a year, if he has either any generosity or any cunning, may create a great dependence by obligations, and still a greater by expectations. Hence we may observe, that, in all free governments, any subject exorbitantly rich has always created jealousy, even though his riches bore no proportion to those of the state. Crassus's fortune, if I remember well, amounted only to about two millions and a half of our money; yet we find, that though his genius was nothing extraordinary, he was able, by means of his riches alone, to counterbalance, during his lifetime, the power of Pompey, as well as that of Cæsar, who afterwards became master of the world. The wealth of the Medici made them masters of Florence, though it is probable it was not considerable, compared to the united property of that opulent republic.

These considerations are apt to make one entertain a magnificent idea of the British spirit and love of liberty, since we could maintain our free government, during so many centuries, against our sovereigns, who, besides the power, and dignity, and majesty of the crown, have always been possessed of much more property than any subject has ever enjoyed in any commonwealth. But it may be said that this spirit, however great, will never be able to support itself against that immense property which is now lodged in the king, and which is still increasing. Upon a moderate computation, there are near three millions a year at the disposal of the crown. The civil list amounts to near a million; the collection of all taxes to another; and the employments in the army and navy, together with ecclesiastical preferments, to above a third million:—an enormous sum, and what may fairly be computed to be more than a thirtieth part of the whole income and labour of the kingdom. When we add to this great property the increasing luxury of the nation, our proneness to corruption, together with the great power and prerogatives of the crown, and the command of military force, there is no one but must despair of being able, without extraordinary efforts, to support our free government much longer under these disadvantages.

On the other hand, those who maintain that the bias of the British government leans towards a republic, may support their opinions by specious arguments. It may be said, that though this immense property in the crown be joined to the dignity of first magistrate, and to many other legal powers and prerogatives, which should naturally give it greater influence; yet it really becomes less dangerous to liberty upon that very account. Were England a republic, and were any private man possessed of a revenue, a third, or even a tenth part as large as that of the crown, he would very justly excite jealousy; because he would infallibly have great authority in the government. And such an irregular authority, not avowed by the laws, is always more dangerous than a much greater authority derived from them. A man possessed of usurped power can set no bounds to his pretensions: his partisans have liberty to hope for every thing in his favour: his enemies provoke his ambition with his fears, by the violence of their opposition: and the government being thrown into a ferment, every corrupted humour in the state naturally gathers to him. On the contrary, a legal authority, though great, has always some bounds, which terminate both the hopes and pretensions of the person possessed of it: the laws must have provided a remedy against its excesses: such an eminent magistrate has much to fear, and little to hope, from his usurpations: and as his legal authority is quietly submitted to, he has small temptation and small opportunity of extending it further. Besides, it happens, with regard to ambitious aims and projects, what may be observed with regard to sects of philosophy and religion. A new sect excites such a ferment, and is both opposed and defended with such vehemence, that it always spreads faster, and multiplies its partisans with greater rapidity than any old established opinion, recommended by the sanction of the laws and of antiquity. Such is the nature of novelty, that, where any thing pleases, it becomes doubly agreeable, if new: but if it displeases, it is doubly displeasing upon that very account. And, in most cases, the violence of enemies is favourable to ambitious projects, as well as the zeal of partisans.

It may further be said, that, though men be much governed by interest, yet even interest itself, and all human affairs, are entirely governed by *opinion*. Now, there has been a sudden and sensible change in the opinions of men within these last fifty years, by the progress of learning and of liberty. Most people in this Island have divested themselves of all superstitious reverence to names and authority: the clergy have much lost their credit: their pretensions and doctrines have been ridiculed; and even religion can scarcely support itself in the world. The mere name of *king* commands little respect; and to talk of a king as God's vicegerent on earth, or to give him any of those magnificent titles which formerly dazzled mankind, would but excite laughter in every one. Though the crown, by means of its large revenue, may maintain its authority, in times of tranquillity, upon private interest and influence, yet, as the least shock or convulsion must break all these interests to pieces, the royal power, being no longer supported by the settled principles and opinions of men, will immediately dissolve. Had men been in the same disposition at the *Revolution*, as they are at present, monarchy would have run a great risk of being entirely lost in this Island.

Durst I venture to deliver my own sentiments amidst these opposite arguments, I would assert, that, unless there happen some extraordinary convulsion, the power of the crown, by means of its large revenue, is rather upon the increase; though at the same time, I own that its progress seems very slow, and almost insensible. The tide has run long, and with some rapidity, to the side of popular government, and is just beginning to turn towards monarchy.

It is well known, that every government must come to a period, and that death is unavoidable to the political, as well as to the animal body. But, as one kind of death may be preferable to another, it may be inquired, whether it be more desirable for the British constitution to terminate in a popular government, or in an absolute monarchy? Here I would frankly declare, that though liberty be preferable to slavery, in almost every case; yet I should rather wish to see an absolute monarch than a republic in this Island. For let us consider what kind of republic we have reason to expect. The question is not concerning any fine imaginary republic, of which a man forms a plan in his closet. There is no doubt but a popular government may be imagined more perfect than an absolute monarchy, or even than our present constitution. But what reason have we to expect that any such government will ever be established in Great Britain, upon the dissolution of our monarchy? If any single person acquire power enough to take our constitution to pieces, and put it up anew, he is really an absolute monarch; and we have already had an instance of this kind, sufficient to convince us, that such a person will never resign his power, or establish any free government. Matters, therefore, must be trusted to their natural progress and operation; and the House of Commons, according to its present constitution, must be the only legislature in such a popular government. The inconveniences attending such a situation of affairs present themselves by thousands. If the House of Commons, in such a case, ever dissolve itself, which is not to be expected, we may look for a civil war every election. If it continue itself, we shall suffer all the tyranny of a faction sub-divided into new factions. And, as such a violent government cannot long subsist, we shall, at last, after many convulsions and civil wars, find repose in absolute monarchy, which it would have been happier for us to have established peaceably from the beginning. Absolute monarchy, therefore, is the easiest death, the true *Euthanasia* of the British constitution.

Thus, if we have reason to be more jealous of monarchy, because the danger is more imminent from that quarter; we have also reason to be more jealous of popular government, because that danger is more terrible. This may teach us a lesson of moderation in all our political controversies.

OF PARTIES IN GENERAL

Of all men that distinguish themselves by memorable achievements, the first place of honour seems due to LEGISLATORS and founders of states, who transmit a system of laws and institutions to secure the peace, happiness, and liberty of future generations. The influence of useful inventions in the arts and sciences may, perhaps, extend further than that of wise laws, whose effects are limited both in time and place; but the benefit arising from the former is not so sensible as that which results from the latter. Speculative sciences do, indeed, improve the mind, but this advantage reaches only to a few persons, who have leisure to apply themselves to them. And as to practical arts, which increase the commodities and enjoyments of life, it is well known that men's happiness consists not so much in an abundance of these, as in the peace and security with which they possess them: and those blessings can only be derived from good government. Not to mention, that general virtue and good morals in a state, which are so requisite to happiness, can never arise from the most refined precepts of philosophy, or even the severest injunctions of religion; but must proceed entirely from the virtuous education of youth, the effect of wise laws and institutions. I must, therefore, presume to differ from Lord Bacon in this particular, and must regard antiquity as somewhat unjust in its distribution of honours, when it made gods of all the inventors of useful arts, such as Ceres, Bacchus, Æsculapius and dignified legislators, such as Romulus and Theseus, only with the appellation of demigods and heroes.

As much as legislators and founders of states ought to be honoured and respected among men, as much ought the founders of sects and factions to be detested and hated; because the influence of faction is directly contrary to that of laws. Factions subvert government, render laws impotent, and beget the fiercest animosities among men of the same nation, who ought to give mutual assistance and protection to each other. And what should render the founders of parties more odious, is the difficulty of extirpating these weeds, when once they have taken root in any state. They naturally propagate themselves for many centuries, and seldom end but by the total dissolution of that government, in which they are sown. They are, besides, plants which grow most plentiful in the richest soil; and though absolute governments be not wholly free from them, it must be confessed, that they rise more easily, and propagate themselves faster in free governments, where they always infect the legislature itself, which alone could be able, by the steady application of rewards and punishments, to eradicate them.

Factions may be divided into Personal and Real; that is, into factions founded on personal friendship or animosity among such as compose the contending parties, and into those founded on some real difference of sentiment or interest. The reason of this distinction is obvious, though I must acknowledge, that parties are seldom found pure and unmixed, either of the one kind or the other. It is not often seen, that a government divides into factions, where there is no difference in the views of the constituent members, either real or apparent, trivial or material: and in those factions, which are founded on the most real and most material difference, there is always observed a great deal of personal animosity or affection. But notwithstanding this mixture, a party may be denominated either personal or real, according to that principle which is predominant, and is found to have the greatest influence.

Personal factions arise most easily in small republics. Every domestic quarrel, there, becomes an affair of state. Love, vanity, emulation, any passion, as well as ambition and resentment, begets public division. The NERI and BIANCHI of Florence, the FREGOSI and ADORNI of Genoa, the COLONNESI and ORSINI of modern Rome, were parties of this kind.

Men have such a propensity to divide into personal factions, that the smallest appearance of real difference will produce them. What can be imagined more trivial than the difference between one colour of livery and another in horse races? Yet this difference begat two most inveterate factions in the Greek empire, the PRASINI and VENETI, who never suspended their animosities till they ruined that unhappy government.

We find in the Roman history a remarkable dissension between two tribes, the POLLIA and PAPIRIA, which continued for the space of near three hundred years, and discovered itself in their suffrages at every election of magistrates. This faction was the more remarkable, as it could continue for so long a tract of time; even though it did not spread itself, nor draw any of the other tribes into a share of the quarrel. If mankind had not a strong propensity to such divisions, the indifference of the rest of the community must have suppressed this foolish animosity, that had not any aliment of new benefits and injuries, of general sympathy and antipathy, which never fail to take place, when the whole state is rent into equal factions.

Nothing is more usual than to see parties, which have begun upon a real difference, continue even after that difference is lost. When men are once enlisted on opposite sides, they contract an affection to the persons with whom they are united, and an animosity against their antagonists; and these passions they often transmit to their posterity. The real difference between Guelf and Ghibelline was long lost in Italy, before these factions were extinguished. The Guelfs adhered to the pope, the Ghibellines to the emperor; yet the family of Sforza, who were in alliance with the emperor, though they were Guelfs, being expelled Milan by the king of France, assisted by Jacomo Trivulzio and the Ghibellines, the pope concurred with the latter, and they formed leagues with the pope against the emperor.

The civil wars which arose some few years ago in Morocco between the *Blacks* and *Whites*, merely on account of their complexion, are founded on a pleasant difference. We laugh at them; but, I believe, were things rightly examined, we afford much more occasion of ridicule to the Moors. For, what are all the wars of religion, which have prevailed in this polite and knowing part of the world? They are certainly more absurd than the Moorish civil wars. The difference of complexion is a sensible and a real difference; but the controversy about an article of faith, which is utterly absurd and unintelligible, is not a difference in sentiment, but in a few phrases and expressions, which one party accepts of without understanding them, and the other refuses in the same manner.[12]

Real factions may be divided into those from *interest*, from *principle*, and from *affection*. Of all factions, the first are the most reasonable, and the most excusable. Where two orders of men, such as the nobles and people, have a distinct authority in a government, not very accurately balanced and modelled, they naturally follow a distinct interest; nor can we reasonably expect a different conduct, considering that degree of selfishness implanted in human nature. It requires great skill in a legislator to prevent such parties; and many philosophers are of opinion, that this secret, like the *grand elixir*, or *perpetual motion*, may amuse men in theory, but can never possibly be reduced to practice. In despotic governments, indeed, factions often do not appear; but they are not the less real; or rather, they are more real and more pernicious upon that very account. The distinct orders of men, nobles and people, soldiers and merchants, have all a distinct interest; but the more powerful oppresses the weaker with impunity, and without resistance; which begets a seeming tranquillity in such governments.

There has been an attempt in England to divide the *landed* and *trading* part of the nation; but without success. The interests of these two bodies are not really distinct, and never will be so, till our public debts increase to such a degree as to become altogether oppressive and intolerable.

Parties from *principle*, especially abstract speculative principle, are known only to modern times, and are, perhaps, the

---

[12] Besides I do not find that the *Whites* in Morocco ever imposed on the Blacks any necessity pi altering their complexion, or frightened them with inquisitions and penal laws in case of obstinacy. Nor have the Blacks been more unreasonable in this particular. But is a man's opinion, where he is able to form a real opinion, more at his disposal than his complexion? And can one be induced by force or fear to do more than paint and disguise in the one case as well as in the other.

most extraordinary and unaccountable *phenomenon* that has yet appeared in human affairs. Where different principles beget a contrariety of conduct, which is the case with all different political principles, the matter may be more easily explained. A man who esteems the true right of government to lie in one man, or one family, cannot easily agree with his fellow-citizen, who thinks that another man or family is possessed of this right. Each naturally wishes that right may take place, according to his own notions of it. But where the difference of principle is attended with no contrariety of action, but every one may follow his own way, without interfering with his neighbour, as happens in all religious controversies, what madness, what fury, can beget such an unhappy and such fatal divisions?

Two men travelling on the highway, the one east, the other west, can easily pass each other, if the way be broad enough: but two men, reasoning upon opposite principles of religion, cannot so easily pass, without shocking, though one should think, that the way were also, in that case, sufficiently broad and that each might proceed, without interruption, in his own course. But such is the nature of the human mind, that it always lays hold on every mind that approaches it; and as it is wonderfully fortified by an unanimity of sentiments, so it is shocked and disturbed by any contrariety. Hence the eagerness which most people discover in a dispute; and hence their impatience of opposition, even in the most speculative and indifferent opinions.

This principle, however frivolous it may appear, seems to have been the origin of all religious wars and divisions. But as this principle is universal in human nature, its effects would not have been confined to one age, and to one sect of religion, did it not there concur with other more accidental causes, which raise it to such a height as to produce the greatest misery and devastation. Most religions of the ancient world arose in the unknown ages of government, when men were as yet barbarous and uninstructed, and the prince, as well as peasant, was disposed to receive, with implicit faith, every pious tale or fiction which was offered him. The magistrate embraced the religion of the people, and, entering cordially into the care of sacred matters, naturally acquired an authority in them, and united the ecclesiastical with the civil power. But the *Christian* religion arising, while principles directly opposite to it were firmly established in the polite part of the world, who despised the nation that first broached this novelty; no wonder that, in such circumstances, it was but little countenanced by the civil magistrate, and that the priesthood was allowed to engross all the authority in the new sect. So bad a use did they make of this power, even in those early times, that the primitive persecutions may, perhaps *in part*,[13] be ascribed to the violence instilled by them into their followers.

And the same principles of priestly government continuing, after Christianity became the established religion, they have engendered a spirit of persecution, which has ever since been the poison of human society, and the source of the most inveterate factions in every government. Such divisions, therefore, on the part of the people, may justly be esteemed factions of *principle*, but, on the part of the priests, who are the prime movers, they are really factions of *interest*.

---

[13] I say *in part*; for it is a vulgar error to imagine, that the ancients were as great friends to toleration as the English or Dutch are at present. The laws against external superstition, among the Romans, were as ancient as the time of the Twelve Tables; and the Jews, as well as Christians, were sometimes punished by them; though, in general, these laws were not rigorously executed. Immediately after the conquest of Gaul, they forbade all but the natives to be initiated into the religion of the Druids; and this was a kind of persecution. In about a century after this conquest, the emperor Claudius quite abolished that superstition by penal laws; which would have been a very grievous persecution, if the imitation of the Roman manners had not, beforehand, weaned the Gauls from their ancient prejudices. Suetonius *in vita Claudii*. Pliny ascribes the abolition of the Druidical superstitions to Tiberius, probably because that emperor had taken some steps towards restraining them (lib. xxx. cap. i). This is an instance of the usual caution and moderation of the Romans in such cases; and very different from their violent and sanguinary method of treating the Christians. Hence we may entertain a suspicion, that those furious persecutions of *Christianity* were in some measure owing to the imprudent zeal and bigotry of the first propagators of that sect; and ecclesiastical history affords us many reasons to confirm this suspicion.

There is another cause (beside the authority of the priests, and the separation of the ecclesiastical and civil powers), which has contributed to render Christendom the scene of religious wars and divisions. Religions that arise in ages totally ignorant and barbarous, consist mostly of traditional tales and fictions, which may be different in every sect, without being contrary to each other; and even when they are contrary, every one adheres to the tradition of his own sect, without much reasoning or disputation. But as philosophy was widely spread over the world at the time when Christianity arose, the teachers of the new sect were obliged to form a system of speculative opinions, to divide, with some accuracy, their articles of faith, and to explain, comment, confute, and defend, with all the subtlety of argument and science. Hence naturally arose keenness in dispute, when the Christian religion came to be split into new divisions and heresies: and this keenness assisted the priests in the policy of begetting a mutual hatred and antipathy among their deluded followers. Sects of philosophy, in the ancient world, were more zealous than parties of religion; but, in modern times, parties of religion are more furious and enraged than the most cruel factions that ever arose from interest and ambition.

I have mentioned parties from *affection* as a kind of *real* parties, beside those from *interest* and *principle*. By parties from affection, I understand those which are founded on the different attachments of men towards particular families and persons whom they desire to rule over them. These factions are often very violent; though, I must own, it may seem unaccountable that men should attach themselves so strongly to persons with whom they are nowise acquainted, whom perhaps they never saw, and from whom they never received, nor can ever hope for, any favour. Yet this we often find to be the case, and even with men, who, on other occasions, discover no great generosity of spirit, nor are found to be easily transported by friendship beyond their own interest. We are apt to think the relation between us and our sovereign very close and intimate. The splendour of majesty and power bestows an importance on the fortunes even of a single person. And when a man's good-nature does not give him this imaginary interest, his ill-nature will, from spite and opposition to persons whose sentiments are different from his own.

OF THE PARTIES OF GREAT BRITAIN

Were the British government proposed as a subject of speculation, one would immediately perceive in it a source of division and party, which it would be almost impossible for it, under any administration, to avoid. The just balance between the republican and monarchical part of our constitution is really in itself so extremely delicate and uncertain, that, when joined to men's passions and prejudices, it is impossible but different opinions must arise concerning it, even among persons of the best understanding. Those of mild tempers, who love peace and order, and detest sedition and civil wars, will always entertain more favourable sentiments of monarchy than men of bold and generous spirits, who are passionate lovers of liberty, and think no evil comparable to subjection and slavery. And though all reasonable men agree in general to preserve our mixed government, yet, when they come to particulars, some will incline to trust greater powers to the crown, to bestow on it more influence, and to guard against its encroachments with less caution, than others who are terrified at the most distant approaches of tyranny and despotic power. Thus are there parties of PRINCIPLE involved in the very nature of our constitution, which may properly enough he denominated those of COURT and COUNTRY.[14] The strength and violence of each of these parties will much depend upon the particular administration. An administration may be so bad, as to throw a great majority into

---

[14] These words have become of general use, and therefore I shall employ them without intending to express by them an universal blame of the one party, or approbation of the other. The Court party may no doubt, on some occasions, consult best the interest of the country, and the Country party oppose it. In like manner, the *Roman* parties were denominated Optimates and Populares; and Cicero, like a true party man, defines the Optimates to be such as, in all their public conduct, regulated themselves by the sentiments of the best and worthiest Romans; *pro Sextio*. The term of Country party may afford a favourable definition or etymology of the same kind; but it would be folly to draw any argument from that head, and I have no regard to it in employing these terms.

the opposition; as a good administration will reconcile to the court many of the most passionate lovers of liberty. But however the nation may fluctuate between them, the parties themselves will always subsist, so long as we are governed by a limited monarchy.

But, besides this difference of *Principle*, those parties are very much fomented by a difference of INTEREST, without which they could scarcely ever be dangerous or violent. The crown will naturally bestow all trust and power upon those whose principles, real or pretended, are most favourable to monarchical government; and this temptation will naturally engage them to go greater lengths than their principles would otherwise carry them. Their antagonists, who are disappointed in their ambitious aims, throw themselves into the party whose sentiments incline them to be most jealous of royal power, and naturally carry those sentiments to a greater height than sound politics will justify. Thus *Court* and *Country*, which are the genuine offspring of the British government, are a kind of mixed parties, and are influenced both by principle and by interest. The heads of the factions are commonly most governed by the latter motive; the inferior members of them by the former.[15]

As to ecclesiastical parties, we may observe, that, in all ages of the world, priests have been enemies to liberty;[16] and, it is certain, that this steady conduct of theirs must have been founded on fixed reasons of interest and ambition. Liberty of thinking, and of expressing our thoughts, is always fatal to priestly power,

---

[15] I must be understood to mean this of persons who have any motive for taking party on any side. For, to tell the truth, the greatest part are commonly men who associate themselves they know not why; from example, from passion, from idleness. But still it is requisite there be some source of division, either in principle or interest; otherwise such persons would not find parties to which they could associate themselves.

[16] This proposition is true, notwithstanding that, in the early times of the English government, the clergy were the great and principal opposers of the crown; but at that time their possessions were so immensely great, that they composed a considerable part of the proprietors of England, and in many contests were direct rivals of the crown.

and to those pious frauds on which it is commonly founded; and, by an infallible connection, which prevails among all kinds of liberty, this privilege can never be enjoyed, at least has never yet been enjoyed, but in a free government. Hence it must happen, in such a constitution as that of Great Britain, that the established clergy, while things are in their natural situation, will always be of the *Court* party; as, on the contrary, dissenters of all kinds will be of the *Country* party; since they can never hope for that toleration which they stand in need of, but by means of our free government. All princes that have aimed at despotic power have known of what importance it was to gain the established clergy; as the clergy, on their part, have shown a great facility in entering into the views of such princes. Gustavus Vasa was, perhaps, the only ambitious monarch that ever depressed the church, at the same time that he discouraged liberty. But the exorbitant power of the bishops in Sweden, who at that time overtopped the crown itself, together with their attachment to a foreign family, was the reason of his embracing such an unusual system of politics.

This observation, concerning propensity of priests to the government of a single person, is not true with regard to one sect only. The *Presbyterian* and *Calvinistic* clergy in Holland, were professed friends to the family of Orange; as the *Arminians*, who were esteemed heretics, were of the Louvestein faction, and zealous for liberty. But if a prince have the choice of both, it is easy to see that he will prefer the Episcopal to the Presbyterian form of government, both because of the greater affinity between monarchy and episcopacy, and because of the facility which he will find, in such a government, of ruling the clergy by means of their ecclesiastical superiors.

If we consider the first rise of parties in England, during the great rebellion, we shall observe that it was conformable to this general theory, and that the species of government gave birth to them by a regular and infallible operation. The English constitution, before that period, had lain in a kind of confusion, yet so as that the subjects possessed many noble privileges, which, though not exactly bounded and secured by law, were universally deemed, from long possession, to belong to them as their birthright. An ambitious, or rather a misguided, prince arose, who deemed all these privileges to be concessions of his predecessors, revocable at pleasure; and, in prosecution of this principle, he openly acted in violation of liberty during the course of several years. Necessity, at last, constrained him to call a parliament; the spirit of liberty arose and spread itself; the prince, being without any support, was obliged to grant every thing required of him; and his enemies, jealous and implacable, set no bounds to their pretensions. Here, then, began those contests in which it was no wonder that men of that age were divided into different parties; since, even at this day, the impartial are at a loss to decide concerning the justice of the quarrel. The pretensions of the parliament, if yielded to, broke the balance of the constitution, by rendering the government almost entirely republican. If not yielded to, the nation was, perhaps, still in danger of absolute power, from the settled principles and inveterate habits of the king, which had plainly appeared in every concession that he had been constrained to make to his people. In this question, so delicate and uncertain, men naturally fell to the side which was most conformable to their usual principles; and the more passionate favourers of monarchy declared for the king, as the zealous friends of liberty sided with the parliament. The hopes of success being nearly equal on both sides, *interest* had no general influence in this contest; so that ROUNDHEAD and CAVALIER were merely parties of principle, neither of which disowned either monarchy or liberty; but the former party inclined most to the republican part of our government, the latter to the monarchical. In this respect, they may be considered as court and country party, inflamed into a civil war, by an unhappy concurrence of circumstances, and by the turbulent spirit of the age. The commonwealth's men, and the partisans of absolute power, lay concealed in both parties, and formed but an inconsiderable part of them.

The clergy had concurred with the king's arbitrary designs; and, in return, were allowed to persecute their adversaries, whom they called heretics and schismatics. The established clergy were Episcopal, the nonconformists Presbyterian; so that all things concurred to throw the former, without reserve, into the king's party, and the latter into that of the parliament.[17]

Every one knows the event of this quarrel; fatal to the king first, to the parliament afterwards. After many confusions and revolutions, the royal family was at last restored, and the ancient government reestablished. Charles II was not made wiser by the example of his father, but prosecuted the same measures, though, at first, with more secrecy and caution. New parties arose, under the appellation of *Whig* and *Tory*, which have continued ever since to confound and distract our government. To determine the nature of these parties is perhaps one of the most difficult problems that can be met with, and is a proof that history may contain questions as uncertain as any to be found in the most abstract sciences. We have seen the conduct of the two parties, during the course of seventy years, in a vast variety of circumstances, possessed of power, and deprived of it, during peace, and during war: persons, who profess themselves of one side or other, we meet with every hour, in company, in our pleasures, in our serious occupations we ourselves are constrained, in a manner, to take party; and, living in a country of the highest liberty, every one may openly declare all the sentiments and

---

[17] The clergy had concurred in a shameless manner with the King's arbitrary designs, according to their usual maxims in such cases, and, in return, were allowed to persecute their adversaries, whom they called heretics and schismatics. The established clergy were Episcopal, the nonconformists Presbyterians; so that all things concurred to throw the former, without reserve, into the King's party, and the latter into that of the Parliament. The *Cavaliers* being the Court party, and the *Roundheads* the Country party, the union was infallible betwixt the former and the established prelacy, and betwixt the latter and Presbyterian nonconformists. This union is so natural, according to the general principles of politics, that it requires some very extraordinary situation of affairs to break it.

opinions: yet are we at a loss to tell the nature, pretensions, and principles, of the different factions.[18]

When we compare the parties of WHIG and TORY with those of ROUNDHEAD and CAVALIER, the most obvious difference that appears between them consists in the principles of *passive obedience*, and *indefeasible right*, which were but little heard of among the Cavaliers, but became the universal doctrine, and were esteemed the true characteristic of a Tory. Were these principles pushed into their most obvious consequences, they imply a formal renunciation of all our liberties, and an avowal of absolute monarchy; since nothing can be greater absurdity than a limited power, which must not be resisted, even when it exceeds its limitations. But, as the most rational principles are often but a weak counterpoise to passion, it is no wonder that these absurd principles were found too weak for that effect. The Tories, as men, were enemies to oppression; and also as Englishmen, they were enemies to arbitrary power. Their zeal for liberty was, perhaps, less fervent than that of their antagonists, but was sufficient to make them forget all their general principles, when they saw themselves openly threatened with a subversion of the ancient government. From these sentiments arose the *Revolution*, an event of mighty consequence, and the firmest foundation of British liberty. The conduct of the Tories during that event, and after it, will afford us a true insight into the nature of that party.

In the *first* place, they appear to have had the genuine sentiments of Britons in their affection for liberty, and in their determined resolution not to sacrifice it to any abstract principle whatsoever, or to any imaginary rights of princes. This part of their character might justly have been doubted of before the Revolution, from the obvious tendency of their avowed principles, and from their compliances with a court, which seemed to make little secret of its arbitrary designs. The Revolution showed them to have been, in this respect, nothing but a genuine *court party*, such as might be expected in a British

---

[18] The question is perhaps in itself somewhat difficult, but has been rendered more so by the prejudices and violence of party.

government; that is, *lovers of liberty, but greater lovers of monarchy*. It must, however, be confessed, that they carried their monarchical principles further even in practice, but more so in theory, than was in any degree consistent with a limited government.

Secondly, Neither their principles nor affections concurred, entirely or heartily, with the settlement made at the *Revolution*, or with that which has since taken place. This part of their character may seem opposite to the former, since any other settlement, in those circumstances of the nation, must probably have been dangerous, if not fatal, to liberty. But the heart of man is made to reconcile contradictions; and this contradiction is not greater than that between *passive obedience* and the *resistance* employed at the Revolution. A TORY, therefore, since the *Revolution*, may be defined, in a few words, to be a *lover of monarchy, though without abandoning liberty, and a partisan of the family of Stuart*: as a WHIG may be defined to be *a lover of liberty, though without renouncing monarchy, and a friend to the settlement in the Protestant line.*[19]

---

[19] The celebrated writer above cited has asserted, that the real distinction betwixt *Whig* and Tory was lost at the *Revolution*, and that ever since they have continued to be mere *personal* parties, like the *Guelfs* and Ghibellines, after the Emperors had lost all authority in Italy. Such an opinion, were it received, would turn our whole history into an enigma.

I shall first mention, as a proof of a real distinction betwixt these parties, what every one may have observed or heard concerning the conduct and conversation of all his friends and acquaintance on both sides. Have not the *Tories* always borne an avowed affection to the family of *Stuart*, and have not their adversaries always opposed with vigour the succession of that family?

The *Tory* principles are confessedly the most favourable to monarchy. Yet the *Tories* have almost always opposed the court these fifty years; nor were they cordial friends to King *William*, even when employed by him. Their quarrel, therefore, cannot be supposed to have lain with the throne, but with the person who sat on it.

They concurred heartily with the court during the four last years of Queen *Anne*. But is any one at a loss to find the reason?

The succession of the crown in the British government is a point of too great consequence to be absolutely indifferent to persons who concern themselves, in any degree, about the fortune of the public; much less can it be supposed that the Tory party, who never valued themselves upon moderation, could maintain a *stoical* indifference in a point of so great importance. Were they, therefore, zealous for the house of *Hanover*? or was there any thing that kept an opposite zeal from openly appearing, if it did not openly appear, but prudence, and a sense of decency?

It is monstrous to see an established Episcopal clergy in declared opposition to the court, and a nonconformist Presbyterian clergy in conjunction with it. What can produce such an unnatural conduct in both? Nothing, but that the former have espoused monarchical principles too high for the present settlement, which is founded on the principles of liberty, and the latter, being afraid of the prevalence of those high principles, adhere to that party from whom they have reason to expect liberty and toleration.

The different conduct of the two parties, with regard to foreign politics, is also a proof to the same purpose. *Holland* has always been most favoured by one, and *France* by the other. In short, the proofs of this kind seem so palpable and evident, that it is almost needless to collect them.

It is however remarkable, that though the principles of *Whig* and *Tory* be both of them of a compound nature, yet the ingredients which predominated in both were not correspondent to each other. A *Tory* loved monarchy, and bore an affection to the family of *Stuart*; but the latter affection was the predominant inclination of the party. A *Whig* loved liberty, and was a friend to the settlement in the Protestant line; but the love of liberty was professedly his predominant inclination. The Tories have frequently acted as republicans, where either policy or revenge has engaged them to that conduct; and there was none of the party who, upon the supposition that they were to be disappointed in their views with regard to the succession, would not have desired to impose the strictest limitations on the crown, and to bring our form of government as near republican as possible, in order to depress the family, that, according to their apprehension, succeeded without any just title. The Whigs, it is true, have also taken steps dangerous to liberty, under pretext of securing the succession and settlement of the crown according to their views; but, as the body of the party had no passion for that succession, otherwise than as the means of securing liberty, they have been betrayed into these steps by ignorance or frailty, or the interest of their leaders. The succession of the crown was, therefore, the chief point with the Tories; the security of our liberties with the Whigs.

It is difficult to penetrate into the thoughts and sentiments of any particular man; but it is almost impossible to distinguish those of a whole party, where it often happens that no two persons agree precisely in the same way of thinking. Yet I will venture to affirm, that it was not so much principle, or an opinion of indefeasible right, that attached the Tories to the ancient family, as affection, or a certain love and esteem for their persons. The same cause divided England formerly betwixt the houses of York and Lancaster, and

These different views, with regard to the settlement of the crown, were accidental, but natural, additions, to the principles of the *Court* and *Country* parties, which are the genuine divisions in

Scotland betwixt the families of Bruce and Baliol, in an age when political disputes were but little in fashion, and when political principles must of course have had but little influence on mankind. The doctrine of passive obedience is so absurd in itself, and so opposite to our liberties, that it seems to have been chiefly left to pulpit declaimers, and to their deluded followers among the *mob* Men of better sense were guided by *affection*, and as to the leaders of this party, it is probable that interest was their sole motive, and that they acted more contrary to their private sentiments than the leaders of the opposite party.

Some who will not venture to assert, that the *real* difference between Whig and Tory, was lost at the *Revolution*, seem inclined to think that the difference is now abolished, and that affairs are so far returned to their natural state, that there are at present no other parties amongst us but *Court* and *Country*; that is, men who, by interest or principle, are attached either to Monarchy or to Liberty. It must indeed be confessed, that the Tory party seem of late to have decayed much in their numbers, still more in their zeal, and I may venture to say, still more in their credit and authority. There are few men of knowledge or learning, at least few philosophers since Mr. Locke has wrote, who would not be ashamed to be thought of that party; and in almost all companies, the name of *Old Whig* is mentioned as an incontestable appellation of honour and dignity. Accordingly, the enemies of the ministry, as a reproach, call the courtiers the true *Tories* and, as an honour, denominate the gentlemen in the Opposition the true *Whigs*.

I shall conclude this subject with observing, that we never had any Tories in Scotland, according to the proper signification of the word, and that the division of parties in this country was really into Whigs and Jacobites. A Jacobite seems to be a Tory, who has no regard to the constitution, but is either a zealous partisan of absolute monarchy, or at least willing to sacrifice our liberties to the obtaining the succession in that family to which he is attached. The reason of the difference betwixt England and Scotland I take to be this. Our political and religious divisions in this country have been, since the Revolution, regularly correspondent to each other. The Presbyterians were all Whigs, without exception; the Episcopalians of the opposite party. And as the clergy of the latter sect were turned out of their churches at the Revolution, they had no motive to make any compliances with the government in their oaths or forms of prayer, but openly avowed the highest principles of their party; which is the cause why their followers have been more barefaced and violent than their brethren of the Tory party in England.

the British Government. A passionate lover of monarchy is apt to be displeased at any change of the succession, as savouring too much of a commonwealth: a passionate lover of liberty is apt to think that every part of the government ought to be subordinate to the interests of liberty.

Some, who will not venture to assert that the *real* difference between Whig and Tory was lost at the *Revolution*, seem inclined to think, that the difference is now abolished, and that affairs are so far returned to their natural state, that there are at present no other parties among us but *Court* and *Country*; that is, men who, by interest or principle, are attached either to monarchy or liberty. The Tories have been so long obliged to talk in the republican style, that they seem to have made converts of themselves by their hypocrisy, and to have embraced the sentiments, as well as language of their adversaries. There are, however, very considerable remains of that party in England, with all their old prejudices; and a proof that *Court* and *Country* are not our only parties, is that almost all the dissenters side with the court, and the lower clergy, at least of the church or England, with the opposition. This may convince us, that some bias still hangs upon our constitution, some extrinsic weight, which turns it from its natural course, and causes a confusion in our parties.[20]

---

[20] Some of the opinions delivered in these Essays, with regard to the public transactions in the last century, the Author, on a more accurate examination, found reason to retract in his History of Great Britain. And as he would not enslave himself to the systems of either party, neither would he fetter his judgment by his own preconceived opinions and principles; nor is he ashamed to acknowledge his mistakes. These mistakes were indeed, at that time almost universal in this kingdom.

OF SUPERSTITION AND ENTHUSIASM

That *the corruption of the best of things produces the worst*, is grown into a maxim, and is commonly proved, among other instances, by the pernicious effects of *superstition* and *enthusiasm*, the corruptions of true religion.

These two species of false religion, though both pernicious, are yet of a very different, and even of a contrary nature. The mind of man is subject to certain unaccountable terrors and apprehensions, proceeding either from the unhappy situation of private or public affairs, from ill health, from a gloomy and melancholy disposition, or from the concurrence of all these circumstances. In such a state of mind, infinite unknown evils are dreaded from unknown agents; and where real objects of terror are wanting, the soul, active to its own prejudice, and fostering its predominant inclination, finds imaginary ones, to whose power and malevolence it sets no limits. As these enemies are entirely invisible and unknown, the methods taken to appease them are equally unaccountable, and consist in ceremonies, observances, mortifications, sacrifices, presents, or in any practice, however absurd or frivolous, which either folly or knavery recommends to a blind and terrified credulity. Weakness, fear, melancholy, together with ignorance, are, therefore, the true sources of Superstition.

But the mind of man is also subject to an unaccountable elevation and presumption, arising from prosperous success, from luxuriant health, from strong spirits, or from a bold and confident disposition. In such a state of mind, the imagination swells with great, but confused conceptions, to which no sublunary beauties or enjoyments can correspond. Every thing mortal and perishable vanishes as unworthy of attention; and a full range is given to the fancy in the invisible regions, or world of Spirits, where the soul is at liberty to indulge itself in every imagination, which may best suit its present taste and disposition. Hence arise raptures, transports, and surprising flights of fancy; and, confidence and presumption still increasing, these raptures, being altogether unaccountable, and seeming quite beyond the reach of our ordinary faculties, are attributed to the immediate inspiration of that Divine Being who is the object of devotion. In a little time, the inspired person comes to regard himself as a distinguished favourite of the Divinity; and when this phrensy once takes place, which is the summit of enthusiasm, every whimsey is consecrated: human reason, and even morality, are rejected as fallacious guides, and the fanatic madman delivers himself over, blindly and without reserve, to the supposed illapses of the Spirit, and to inspiration from above. Hope, pride, presumption, a warm imagination, together with ignorance, are therefore the true sources of Enthusiasm.

These two species of false religion might afford occasion to many speculations, but I shall confine myself, at present, to a few reflections concerning their different influence on government and society.

My *first* reflection is, *that superstition is favourable to priestly power, and enthusiasm not less, or rather more contrary to it, than sound reason and philosophy.* As superstition is founded on fear, sorrow, and a depression of spirits, it represents the man to himself in such despicable colours, that he appears unworthy, in his own eyes, of approaching the Divine presence, and naturally has recourse to any other person, whose sanctity of life, or perhaps impudence and cunning, have made him be supposed more favoured by the Divinity. To him the superstitious intrust their devotions to his care they recommend their prayers, petitions, and sacrifices: and by his means, they hope to render their addresses acceptable to their incensed Deity. Hence the origin of Priests, who may justly be regarded as an invention of a timorous and abject superstition, which, ever diffident of itself, dares not offer up its own devotions, but ignorantly thinks to recommend itself to the Divinity, by the mediation of his supposed friends and servants. As superstition is a considerable ingredient in almost all religions, even the most fanatical; there being nothing but philosophy able entirely to conquer these unaccountable terrors; hence it proceeds, that in almost every sect of religion there are priests to be found: but the stronger mixture there is of superstition, the higher is the authority of the priesthood.

On the other hand, it may be observed, that all enthusiasts have been free from the yoke of ecclesiastics, and have expressed great independence in their devotion, with a contempt of forms, ceremonies, and traditions. The *Quakers* are the most egregious, though, at the same time, the most innocent enthusiasts that have yet been known; and are perhaps the only sect that have never admitted priests among them. The *Independents*, of all the English sectaries, approach nearest to the *Quakers* in fanaticism, and in their freedom from priestly bondage. The *Presbyterians* follow after, at an equal distance, in both particulars. In short, this observation is founded in experience; and will also appear to be founded in reason, if we consider, that, as enthusiasm arises from a presumptuous pride and confidence, it thinks itself sufficiently qualified to *approach* the Divinity, without any human mediator. Its rapturous devotions are so fervent, that it even imagines itself *actually* to *approach* him by the way of contemplation and inward converse; which makes it neglect all those outward ceremonies and observances, to which the assistance of the priests appears so requisite in the eyes of their superstitious votaries. The fanatic consecrates himself, and bestows on his own person a sacred character, much superior to what forms and ceremonious institutions can confer on any other.

My *second* reflection with regard to these species of false religion is, *that religions which partake of enthusiasm, are, on their first rise, more furious and violent than those which partake of superstition; but in a little time become more gentle and moderate.* The violence of this species of religion, when excited by novelty, and animated by opposition, appears from numberless instances; of the *Anabaptists* in Germany, the *Camisars* in France, the *Levellers*, and other fanatics in England, and the *Covenanters* in Scotland. Enthusiasm being founded on strong spirits, and a presumptuous boldness of character, it naturally begets the most extreme resolutions; especially after it rises to that height as to inspire the deluded fanatic with the opinion of Divine illuminations, and with a contempt for the common rules of reason, morality, and prudence.

It is thus enthusiasm produces the most cruel disorders in human society; but its fury is like that of thunder and tempest, which exhaust themselves in a little time, and leave the air more calm and serene than before. When the first fire of enthusiasm is spent, men naturally, in all fanatical sects, sink into the greatest remissness and coolness in sacred matters; there being no body of men among them endowed with sufficient authority, whose interest is concerned to support the religious spirit; no rites, no ceremonies, no holy observances, which may enter into the common train of life, and preserve the sacred principles from oblivion. Superstition, on the contrary, steals in gradually and insensibly; renders men tame and submissive; is acceptable to the magistrate, and seems inoffensive to the people: till at last the priest, having firmly established his authority, becomes the tyrant and disturber of human society, by his endless contentions, persecutions, and religious wars. How smoothly did the Romish church advance in her acquisition of power! But into what dismal convulsions did she throw all Europe, in order to maintain it! On the other hand, our sectaries, who were formerly such dangerous bigots, are now become very free reasoners; and the *Quakers* seem to approach nearly the only regular body of *Deists* in the universe, the *literati* or the disciples of Confucius in China.[21]

My *third* observation on this head is, *that superstition is an enemy to civil liberty, and enthusiasm a friend to it*. As superstition groans under the dominion of priests, and enthusiasm is destructive of all ecclesiastical power, this sufficiently accounts for the present observation. Not to mention that enthusiasm, being the infirmity of bold and ambitious tempers, is naturally accompanied with a spirit of liberty, as superstition, on the contrary, renders men tame and abject, and fits them for slavery. We learn from English history, that, during the civil wars, the

---

[21] The Chinese literati have no priests or ecclesiastical establishment.

Independents and *Deists*, though the most opposite in their religious principles, yet were united in their political ones, and were alike passionate for a commonwealth. And since the origin of *Whig* and *Tory*, the leaders of the *Whigs* have either been *Deists* or professed *Latitudinarians* in their principles; that is, friends to toleration, and indifferent to any particular sect of *Christians*: while the sectaries, who have all a strong tincture of enthusiasm, have always, without exception, concurred with that party in defence of civil liberty. The resemblance in their superstitions long united the High-Church *Tories* and the *Roman Catholics*, in support of prerogative and kingly power, though experience of the tolerating spirit of the *Whigs* seems of late to have reconciled the *Catholics* to that party.

The *Molinists* and *Jansenists* in France have a thousand unintelligible disputes, which are not worthy the reflection of a man of sense: but what principally distinguishes these two sects, and alone merits attention, is the different spirit of their religion. The *Molinists*, conducted by the *Jesuits*, are great friends to superstition, rigid observers of external forms and ceremonies, and devoted to the authority of the priests, and to tradition. The *Jansenists* are enthusiasts, and zealous promoters of the passionate devotion, and of the inward life, little influenced by authority, and, in a word, but half Catholics. The consequences are exactly conformable to the foregoing reasoning. The *Jesuits* are the tyrants of the people, and the slaves of the court; and the *Jansenists* preserve alive the small sparks of the love of liberty which are to be found in the French nation.

OF THE DIGNITY OR MEANNESS OF HUMAN NATURE

There are certain sects which secretly form themselves in the learned world, as well as factions in the political; and though sometimes they come not to an open rupture, they give a different turn to the ways of thinking of those who have taken part on either side. The most remarkable of this kind are the sects founded on the different sentiments with regard to the *dignity of human nature*; which is a point that seems to have divided philosophers and poets, as well as divines, from the beginning of the world to this day. Some exalt our species to the skies, and represent man as a kind of human demigod, who derives his origin from heaven, and retains evident marks of his lineage and descent. Others insist upon the blind sides of human nature, and can discover nothing, except vanity, in which man surpasses the other animals, whom he affects so much to despise. If an author possess the talent of rhetoric and declamation, he commonly takes part with the former: if his turn lie towards irony and ridicule, he naturally throws himself into the other extreme.

I am far from thinking that all those who have depreciated our species have been enemies to virtue, and have exposed the frailties of their fellow-creatures with any bad intention. On the contrary, I am sensible that a delicate sense of morals, especially when attended with a splenetic temper, is apt to give a man a disgust of the world, and to make him consider the common course of human affairs with too much indignation. I must, however, be of opinion, that the sentiments of those who are inclined to think favourably of mankind, are more advantageous to virtue than the contrary principles, which give us a mean opinion of our nature. When a man is prepossessed with a high notion of his rank and character in the creation, he will naturally endeavour to act up to it, and will scorn to do a base or vicious action which might sink him below that figure which he makes in his own imagination. Accordingly, we find, that all our polite and fashionable moralists insist upon this topic, and endeavour to represent vice unworthy of man, as well as odious in itself.[22]

We find new disputes that are not founded on some ambiguity in the expression; and I am persuaded that the present dispute, concerning the dignity or meanness of human nature, is not more exempt from it than any other. It may therefore be worth while to consider what is real, and what is only verbal, in this controversy.

That there is a natural difference between merit and demerit, virtue and vice, wisdom and folly, no reasonable man will deny, yet it is evident that, in affixing the term, which denotes either our approbation or blame, we are commonly more influenced by comparison than by any fixed unalterable standard in the nature of things. In like manner, quantity, and extension, and bulk, are by every one acknowledged to be real things: but when we call any animal *great* or *little*, we always form a secret comparison between that animal and others of the same species; and it is that comparison which regulates our judgment concerning its greatness. A dog and a horse may be of the very same size, while the one is admired for the greatness of its bulk, and the other for the smallness. When I am present, therefore, at any dispute, I always consider with myself whether it be a question of comparison or not that is the subject of controversy; and if it be, whether the disputants compare the same objects together, or talk of things that are widely different.

In forming our notions of human nature, we are apt to make a comparison between men and animals, the only creatures endowed with thought that fall under our senses. Certainly this comparison is favourable to mankind. On the one hand, we see a creature whose thoughts are not limited by any narrow bounds, either of place or time; who carries his researches into the most distant regions of this globe, and beyond this globe, to the planets

---

[22] Women are generally much more flattered in their youth than men, which may proceed from this reason among others, that their chief point of honour is considered as much more difficult than ours, and requires to be supported by all that decent pride which can be instilled into them.

and heavenly bodies; looks backward to consider the first origin, at least the history of the human race; casts his eye forward to see the influence of his actions upon posterity and the judgments which will be formed of his character a thousand years hence; a creature, who traces causes and effects to a great length and intricacy, extracts general principles from particular appearances; improves upon his discoveries; corrects his mistakes; and makes his very errors profitable. On the other hand, we are presented with a creature the very reverse of this; limited in its observations and reasonings to a few sensible objects which surround it; without curiosity, without foresight; blindly conducted by instinct, and attaining, in a short time, its utmost perfection, beyond which it is never able to advance a single step. What a wide difference is there between these creatures! And how exalted a notion must we entertain of the former, in comparison of the latter.

There are two means commonly employed to destroy this conclusion: *First*, By making an unfair representation of the case, and insisting only upon the weakness of human nature. And, *secondly*, By forming a new and secret comparison between man and beings of the most perfect wisdom. Among the other excellences of man, this is one, that he can form an idea of perfections much beyond what he has experience of in himself; and is not limited in his conception of wisdom and virtue. He can easily exalt his notions, and conceive a degree of knowledge, which, when compared to his own, will make the latter appear very contemptible, and will cause the difference between that and the sagacity of animals, in a manner, to disappear and vanish. Now this being a point in which all the world is agreed, that human understanding falls infinitely short of perfect wisdom, it is proper we should know when this comparison takes place, that we may not dispute where there is no real difference in our sentiments. Man falls much more short of perfect wisdom, and even of his own ideas of perfect wisdom, than animals do of man; yet the latter difference is so considerable, that nothing but a comparison with the former can make it appear of little moment.

It is also usual to *compare* one man with another; and finding very few whom we can call *wise* or *virtuous*, we are apt to entertain a contemptible notion of our species in general. That we may be sensible of the fallacy of this way of reasoning, we may observe, that the honourable appellations of wise and virtuous are not annexed to any particular degree of those qualities of *wisdom* and *virtue*, but arise altogether from the comparison we make between one man and another. When we find a man who arrives at such a pitch of wisdom, as is very uncommon, we pronounce him a wise man: so that to say there are few wise men in the world, is really to say nothing; since it is only by their scarcity that they merit that appellation. Were the lowest of our species as wise as Tully or Lord Bacon, we should still have reason to say that there are few wise men. For in that case we should exalt our notions of wisdom, and should not pay a singular homage to any one who was not singularly distinguished by his talents. In like manner, I have heard it observed by thoughtless people, that there are few women possessed of beauty in comparison of those who want it; not considering that we bestow the epithet of *beautiful* only on such as possess a degree of beauty that is common to them with a few. The same degree of beauty in a woman is called deformity, which is treated as real beauty in one of our sex.

As it is usual, in forming a notion of our species, to *compare* it with the other species above or below it, or to compare the individuals of the species among themselves; so we often compare together the different motives or actuating principles of human nature, in order to regulate our judgment concerning it. And, indeed, this is the only kind of comparison which is worth our attention, or decides any thing in the present question. Were our selfish and vicious principles so much predominant above our social and virtuous, as is asserted by some philosophers, we ought undoubtedly to entertain a contemptible notion of human nature.[23]

---

[23] I may perhaps treat more fully of this subject in some future Essay. In the meantime I shall observe, what has been proved beyond question by several great moralists of the present age, that the social passions are by far the most

There is much of a dispute of words in all this controversy. When a man denies the sincerity of all public spirit or affection to a country and community, I am at a loss what to think of him. Perhaps he never felt this passion in so clear and distinct a manner as to remove all his doubts concerning its force and reality. But when he proceeds afterwards to reject all private friendship, if no interest or self-love intermix itself; I am then confident that he abuses terms, and confounds the ideas of things; since it is impossible for any one to be so selfish, or rather so stupid, as to make no difference between one man and another, and give no preference to qualities which engage his approbation and esteem. Is he also, say I, as insensible to anger as he pretends to be to friendship? And does injury and wrong no more affect him than kindness or benefits? Impossible: he does not know himself: he has forgotten the movements of his heart; or rather, he makes use of a different language from the rest of his countrymen and calls not things by their proper names. What say you of natural affection? (I subjoin), Is that also a species of self-love? Yes; all is self-love. *Your* children are loved only because they are yours: *your* friend for a like reason; and *your* country engages you only so far as it has a connection with *yourself*. Were the idea of self removed, nothing would affect you: you would be altogether unactive and insensible: or, if you ever give yourself any movement, it would only be from vanity, and a desire of fame and reputation to this same self. I am willing, reply I, to receive your interpretation of human actions, provided you admit the facts. That species of self-love which displays itself in kindness to others, you must allow to have great influence over human actions, and even greater, on many occasions, than that which remains in its original shape and form. For how few are there, having a family, children, and relations, who do not spend more

---

powerful of any, and that even all the other passions, receive from them their chief force and influence. Whoever desires to see this question treated at large, with the greatest force of argument and eloquence, may consult my Lord Shaftesbury's Enquiry concerning Virtue.

on the maintenance and education of these than on their own pleasures? This, indeed, you justly observe, may proceed from their self-love, since the prosperity of their family and friends is one, or the chief of their pleasures, as well as their chief honour. Be you also one of these selfish men, and you are sure of every one's good opinion and good-will; or, not to shock your ears with their expressions, the self-love of every one, and mine among the rest, will then incline us to serve you, and speak well of you.

In my opinion, there are two things which have led astray those philosophers that have insisted so much on the selfishness of man. In the *first* place, they found that every act of virtue or friendship was attended with a secret pleasure; whence they concluded, that friendship and virtue could not be disinterested. But the fallacy of this is obvious. The virtuous sentiment or passion produces the pleasure, and does not arise from it. I feel a pleasure in doing good to my friend, because I love him; but do not love him for the sake of that pleasure.

In the *second* place, it has always been found, that the virtuous are far from being indifferent to praise; and therefore they have been represented as a set of vainglorious men, who had nothing in view but the applauses of others. But this also is a fallacy. It is very unjust in the world, when they find any tincture of vanity in a laudable action, to depreciate it upon that account, or ascribe it entirely to that motive. The case is not the same with vanity, as with other passions. Where avarice or revenge enters into any seemingly virtuous action, it is difficult for us to determine how far it enters, and it is natural to suppose it the sole actuating principle. But vanity is so closely allied to virtue, and to love the fame of laudable actions approaches so near the love of laudable actions for their own sake, that these passions are more capable of mixture, than any other kinds of affection; and it is almost impossible to have the latter without some degree of the former. Accordingly we find, that this passion for glory is always warped and varied according to the particular taste or disposition of the mind on which it falls. Nero had the same vanity in driving a chariot, that Trajan had in governing the empire with justice and ability. To love the glory of virtuous deeds is a sure proof of the love of virtue.

OF CIVIL LIBERTY

Those who employ their pens on political subjects, free from party rage, and party prejudices, cultivate a science, which, of all others, contributes most to public utility, and even to the private satisfaction of those who addict themselves to the study of it. I am apt, however, to entertain a suspicion, that the world is still too young to fix many general truths in politics, which will remain true to the latest posterity. We have not as yet had experience of three thousand years; so that not only the art of reasoning is still imperfect in this science, as in all others, but we even want sufficient materials upon which we can reason. It is not fully known what degree of refinement, either in virtue or vice, human nature is susceptible of, nor what may be expected of mankind from any great revolution in their education, customs, or principles. Machiavel was certainly a great genius; but, having confined his study to the furious and tyrannical governments of ancient times, or to the little disorderly principalities of Italy, his reasonings, especially upon monarchical government, have been found extremely defective; and there scarcely is any maxim in his *Prince* which subsequent experience has not entirely refuted. 'A weak prince,' says he, 'is incapable of receiving good counsel; for, if he consult with several, he will not be able to choose among their different counsels. If he abandon himself to one, that minister may perhaps have capacity, but he will not long be a minister. He will be sure to dispossess his master, and place himself and his family upon the throne.' I mention this, among many instances of the errors of that politician, proceeding, in a great measure, from his having lived in too early an age of the world, to be a good judge of political truth. Almost all the princes of Europe are at present governed by their ministers, and have been so for near two centuries, and yet no such event has ever happened, or can possibly happen. Sejanus might project dethroning the Cæsars, but Fleury, though ever so vicious, could not, while in his senses, entertain the least hopes of dispossessing the Bourbons.

Trade was never esteemed an affair of state till the last century; and there scarcely is any ancient writer on politics who has made mention of it. Even the Italians have kept a profound silence with regard to it, though it has now engaged the chief attention, as well of ministers of state, as of speculative reasoners. The great opulence, grandeur, and military achievements of the two maritime powers, seem first to have instructed mankind in the importance of an extensive commerce.

Having therefore intended, in this Essay, to make a full comparison of civil liberty and absolute government, and to show the great advantages of the former above the latter; I began to entertain a suspicion that no man in this age was sufficiently qualified for such an undertaking, and that, whatever any one should advance on that head, would in all probability be refuted by further experience, and be rejected by posterity. Such mighty revolutions have happened in human affairs, and so many events have arisen contrary to the expectation of the ancients, that they are sufficient to beget the suspicion of still further changes.

It had been observed by the ancients, that all the arts and sciences arose among free nations; and that the Persians and Egyptians, notwithstanding their ease, opulence, and luxury, made but faint efforts towards a relish in those finer pleasures, which were carried to such perfection by the Greeks, amidst continual wars, attended with poverty, and the greatest simplicity of life and manners. It had also been observed, that, when the Greeks lost their liberty, though they increased mightily in riches by means of the conquests of Alexander, yet the arts, from that moment, declined among them, and have never since been able to raise their head in that climate. Learning was transplanted to Rome, the only free nation at that time in the universe; and having met with so favourable a soil, it made prodigious shoots for above a century; till the decay of liberty produced also the decay of letters, and spread a total barbarism over the world. From these two experiments, of which, each was double in its kind, and showed the fall of learning in absolute governments, as well as its rise in popular ones, Longinus thought himself sufficiently justified in asserting that the arts and sciences could never flourish but in a free government. And in this opinion he has been followed by several eminent writers[24] in our own country, who either confined their view merely to ancient facts, or entertained too great a partiality in favour of that form of government established among us.

But what would these writers have said to the instances of modern Rome and Florence? Of which the former carried to perfection all the finer arts of sculpture, painting, and music, as well as poetry, though it groaned under tyranny, and under the tyranny of priests, while the latter made its chief progress in the arts and sciences after it began to lose its liberty by the usurpation of the family of Medici. Ariosto, Tasso, Galileo, no more than Raphael or Michael Angelo, were born in republics. And though the Lombard school was famous as well as the Roman, yet the Venetians have had the smallest share in its honours, and seem rather inferior to the other Italians in their genius for the arts and sciences. Rubens established his school at Antwerp, not at Amsterdam. Dresden, not Hamburg, is the centre of politeness in Germany.

But the most eminent instance of the flourishing of learning in absolute governments is that of France, which scarcely ever enjoyed any established liberty, and yet has carried the arts and sciences as near perfection as any other nation. The English are, perhaps, greater philosophers; the Italians better painters and musicians; the Romans were greater orators; but the French are the only people, except the Greeks, who have been at once philosophers, poets, orators, historians, painters, architects, sculptors, and musicians. With regard to the stage, they have excelled even the Greeks, who far excelled the English. And, in common life, they have, in a great measure, perfected that art, the most useful and agreeable of any, *l'Art de Vivre*, the art of society and conversation.

---

[24] Mr. Addison and Lord Shaftesbury.

If we consider the state of the sciences and polite arts in our own country, Horace's observation, with regard to the Romans, may in a great measure be applied to the British.

> Sed in longum tamen ævum
> Manserunt, hodieque manent *vestigia ruris.*

The elegance and propriety of style have been very much neglected among us. We have no dictionary of our language, and scarcely a tolerable grammar. The first polite prose we have was writ by a man who is still alive.[25] As to Sprat, Locke, and even Temple, they knew too little of the rules of art to be esteemed elegant writers. The prose of Bacon, Harrington, and Milton, is altogether stiff and pedantic, though their sense be excellent. Men, in this country, have been so much occupied in the great disputes of *Religion, Politics,* and *Philosophy,* that they had no relish for the seemingly minute observations of grammar and criticism. And, though this turn of thinking must have considerably improved our sense and our talent of reasoning, it must be confessed, that even in those sciences above mentioned, we have not any standard book which we can transmit to posterity: and the utmost we have to boast of, are a few essays towards a more just philosophy, which indeed promise well, but have not as yet reached any degree of perfection.

It has become an established opinion, that commerce can never flourish but in a free government; and this opinion seems to be founded on a longer and larger experience than the foregoing, with regard to the arts and sciences. If we trace commerce in its progress through Tyre, Athens, Syracuse, Carthage, Venice, Florence, Genoa, Antwerp, Holland, England, &c., we shall always find it to have fixed its seat in free governments. The three greatest trading towns now in Europe, are London, Amsterdam, and Hamburg; all free cities, and Protestant cities; that is, enjoying a double liberty. It must, however, be observed, that the

---

[25] Dr. Swift.

great jealousy entertained of late with regard to the commerce of France, seems to prove that this maxim is no more certain and infallible than the foregoing, and that the subjects of an absolute prince may become our rivals in commerce as well as in learning.

Durst I deliver my opinion in an affair of so much uncertainty, I would assert, that notwithstanding the efforts of the French, there is something hurtful to commerce inherent in the very nature of absolute government, and inseparable from it; though the reason I should assign for this opinion is somewhat different from that which is commonly insisted on. Private property seems to me almost as secure in a civilized European monarchy as in a republic, nor is danger much apprehended, in such a government, from the violence of the sovereign, more than we commonly dread harm from thunder, or earthquakes, or any accident the most unusual and extraordinary. Avarice, the spur of industry, is so obstinate a passion, and works its way through so many real dangers and difficulties, that it is not likely to be scared by an imaginary danger, which is so small, that it scarcely admits of calculation. Commerce, therefore, in my opinion, is apt to decay in absolute governments, not because it is there less secure, but because it is less *honourable*. A subordination of rank is absolutely necessary to the support of monarchy. Birth, titles, and place, must be honoured above industry and riches; and while these notions prevail, all the considerable traders will be tempted to throw up their commerce, in order to purchase some of those employments, to which privileges and honours are annexed.

Since I am upon this head, of the alterations which time has produced, or may produce in politics, I must observe, that all kinds of government, free and absolute, seem to have undergone in modern times, a great change for the better, with regard both to foreign and domestic management. The *balance* of power is a secret in politics, fully known only to the present age; and I must add, that the internal police of states has also received great improvements within the last century. We are informed by Sallust, that Catiline's army was much augmented by the accession of the highwaymen about Rome; though I believe, that all of that profession who are at present dispersed over Europe would not amount to a regiment. In Cicero's pleadings for Milo, I find this argument, among others, made use of to prove that his client had not assassinated Clodius. Had Milo, said he, intended to have killed Clodius, he had not attacked him in the daytime, and at such a distance from the city; he had waylaid him at night, near the suburbs, where it might have been pretended that he was killed by robbers; and the frequency of the accident would have favoured the deceit. This is a surprising proof of the loose policy of Rome, and of the number and force of these robbers, since Clodius was at that time attended by thirty slaves, who were completely armed, and sufficiently accustomed to blood and danger in the frequent tumults excited by that seditious tribune.

But though all kinds of government be improved in modern times, yet monarchical government seems to have made the greatest advances towards perfection. It may now be affirmed of civilized monarchies, what was formerly said in praise of republics alone, *that they are a government of Laws, not of Men*. They are found susceptible of order, method, and constancy, to a surprising degree. Property is there secure, industry encouraged, the arts flourish, and the prince lives secure among his subjects, like a father among his children. There are, perhaps, and have been for two centuries, near two hundred absolute princes, great and small, in Europe; and allowing twenty years to each reign, we may suppose, that there have been in the whole two thousand monarchs, or tyrants, as the Greeks would have called them; yet of these there has not been one, not even Philip II of Spain, so bad as Tiberius, Caligula, Nero, or Domitian, who were four in twelve among the Roman emperors. It must, however, be confessed, that though monarchical governments have approached nearer to popular ones in gentleness and stability, they are still inferior. Our modern education and customs instil more humanity and moderation than the ancient; but have not as yet been able to overcome entirely the disadvantages of that form of government.

But here I must beg leave to advance a conjecture, which seems probable, but which posterity alone can fully judge of. I am apt to think, that in monarchical governments there is a source of improvement, and in popular governments a source of degeneracy, which in time will bring these species of civil polity still nearer an equality. The greatest abuses which arise in France, the most perfect model of pure monarchy, proceed not from the number or weight of the taxes, beyond what are to be met with in free countries; but from the expensive, unequal, arbitrary, and intricate method of levying them, by which the industry of the poor, especially of the peasants and farmers, is in a great measure discouraged, and agriculture rendered a beggarly and slavish employment. But to whose advantage do these abuses tend? If to that of the nobility, they might be esteemed inherent in that form of government, since the nobility are the true supports of monarchy; and it is natural their interest should be more consulted in such a constitution, than that of the people. But the nobility are, in reality, the chief losers by this oppression, since it ruins their estates, and beggars their tenants. The only gainers by it are the *Financiers*, a race of men rather odious to the nobility and the whole kingdom. If a prince or minister, therefore, should arise, endowed with sufficient discernment to know his own and the public interest, and with sufficient force of mind to break through ancient customs, we might expect to see these abuses remedied; in which case, the difference between that absolute government and our free one would not appear so considerable as at present.

The source of degeneracy which may be remarked in free governments, consists in the practice of contracting debt, and mortgaging the public revenues, by which taxes may, in time, become altogether intolerable, and all the property of the state be brought into the hands of the public The practice is of modern date. The Athenians, though governed by a republic, paid near two hundred per cent. for those sums of money which any emergence made it necessary for them to borrow; as we learn from Xenophon. Among the moderns, the Dutch first introduced the practice of borrowing great sums at low interest, and have wellnigh ruined themselves by it. Absolute princes have also contracted debt; but as an absolute prince may make a bankruptcy when he pleases, his people can never be oppressed by his debts. In popular governments, the people, and chiefly those who have the highest offices, being commonly the public creditors, it is difficult for the state to make use of tills remedy, which, however it may sometimes be necessary, is always cruel and barbarous. This, therefore, seems to be an inconvenience which nearly threatens all free governments, especially our own, at the present juncture of affairs. And what a strong motive is this to increase our frugality of public money, lest, for want of it, we be reduced, by the multiplicity of taxes, or, what is worse, by our public impotence and inability for defence, to curse our very liberty, and wish ourselves in the same state of servitude with all the nations who surround us?

OF ELOQUENCE

Those who consider the periods and revolutions of human kind, as represented in history, are entertained with a spectacle full of pleasure and variety, and see with surprise the manners, customs, and opinions of the same species susceptible of such prodigious changes in different periods of time. It may, however, be observed, that, in *civil* history, there is found a much greater uniformity than in the history of learning and science, and that the wars, negotiations, and politics of one age, resemble more those of another than the taste, wit, and speculative principles. Interest and ambition, honour and shame, friendship and enmity, gratitude and revenge, are the prime movers in all public transactions; and these passions are of a very stubborn and untractable nature, in comparison of the sentiments and understanding, which are easily varied by education and example. The Goths were much more inferior to the Romans in taste and science than in courage and virtue.

But not to compare together nations so widely different, it may be observed, that even this latter period of human learning is, in many respects, of an opposite character to the ancient; and that, if we be superior in philosophy, we are still, notwithstanding all our refinements, much inferior in eloquence.

In ancient times, no work of genius was thought to require so great parts and capacity as the speaking in public; and some eminent writers have pronounced the talents even of a great poet or philosopher to be of an inferior nature to those which are requisite for such an undertaking. Greece and Rome produced, each of them, but one accomplished orator; and, whatever praises the other celebrated speakers might merit, they were still esteemed much inferior to those great models of eloquence. It is observable, that the ancient critics could scarcely find two orators in any age who deserved to be placed precisely in the same rank, and possessed the same degree of merit. Calvus, Cælius, Curio, Hortensius, Cæsar, rose one above another: but the greatest of that age was inferior to Cicero, the most eloquent speaker that had ever appeared in Rome. Those of fine taste, however, pronounced this judgment of the Roman orator, as well as of the Grecian, that both of them surpassed in eloquence all that had ever appeared, but that they were far from reaching the perfection of their art, which was infinite, and not only exceeded human force to attain, but human imagination to conceive. Cicero declares himself dissatisfied with his own performances, nay, even with those of Demosthenes. *Ita sunt avidæ et capaces meæ aures,* says he, *et semper aliquid immensum infinitumque desiderant.*

Of all the polite and learned nations, England alone possesses a popular government, or admits into the legislature such numerous assemblies as can be supposed to lie under the dominion of eloquence. But what has England to boast of in this particular? In enumerating the great men who have done honour to our country, we exult in our poets and philosophers; but what orators are ever mentioned? or where are the monuments of their genius to be met with? There are found, indeed, in our histories, the names of several, who directed the resolutions of our parliament: but neither themselves nor others have taken the pains to preserve their speeches, and the authority, which they possessed, seems to have been owing to their experience, wisdom, or power, more than to their talents for oratory. At present there are above half a dozen speakers in the two Houses, who, in the judgment of the public, have reached very near the same pitch of eloquence; and no man pretends to give any one the preference above the rest. This seems to me a certain proof, that none of them have attained much beyond a mediocrity in their art, and that the species of eloquence, which they aspire to, gives no exercise to the sublimer faculties of the mind, but may be reached by ordinary talents and a slight application. A hundred cabinet-makers in London can work a table or a chair equally well; but no one poet can write verses with such spirit and elegance as Mr. Pope.

We are told, that, when Demosthenes was to plead, all ingenious men flocked to Athens from the most remote parts of Greece, as to the most celebrated spectacle of the world. At

London, you may see men sauntering in the court of requests, while the most important debate is carrying on in the two Houses; and many do not think themselves sufficiently compensated for the losing of their dinners, by all the eloquence of our most celebrated speakers. When old Cibber is to act, the curiosity of several is more excited, than when our prime minister is to defend himself from a motion for his removal or impeachment.

Even a person, unacquainted with the noble remains of ancient orators, may judge, from a few strokes, that the style or species of their eloquence was infinitely more sublime than that which modern orators aspire to. How absurd would it appear, in our temperate and calm speakers, to make use of an *Apostrophe*, like that noble one of Demosthenes, so much celebrated by Quintilian and Longinus, when, justifying the unsuccessful battle of Chæronea, he breaks out, 'No, my fellow-citizens. No: you have not erred. I swear by the *manes* of those heroes, who fought for the same cause in the plains of Marathon and Platæa.' Who could now endure such a bold and poetical figure as that which Cicero employs, after describing, in the most tragical terms, the crucifixion of a Roman citizen? 'Should I paint the horrors of this scene, not to Roman citizens, not to the allies of our state, not to those who have ever heard of the Roman name, not even to men, but to brute creatures; or, to go further, should I lift up my voice in the most desolate solitude, to the rocks and mountains, yet should I surely see those rude and inanimate parts of nature moved with horror and indignation at the recital of so enormous an action.' With what a blaze of eloquence must such a sentence be surrounded to give it grace, or cause it to make any impression on the hearers! And what noble art and sublime talents are requisite to arrive, by just degrees, at a sentiment so bold and excessive! To inflame the audience, so as to make them accompany the speaker in such violent passions, and such elevated conceptions; and to conceal, under a torrent of eloquence, the artifice by which all this is effectuated! Should this sentiment even appear to us excessive, as perhaps justly it may, it will at least serve to give an idea of the style of ancient eloquence, where such swelling expressions were not rejected as wholly monstrous and gigantic.

Suitable to this vehemence of thought and expression, was the vehemence of action, observed in the ancient orators. The *supplosio pedis*, or stamping with the foot, was one of the most usual and moderate gestures which they made use of; though that is now esteemed too violent, either for the senate, bar, or pulpit, and is only admitted into the theatre to accompany the most violent passions which are there represented.

One is somewhat at a loss to what cause we may ascribe so sensible a decline of eloquence in latter ages. The genius of mankind, at all times, is perhaps equal: the moderns have applied themselves, with great industry and success, to all the other arts and sciences: and a learned nation possesses a popular government; a circumstance which seems requisite for the full display of these noble talents: but notwithstanding all these advantages, our progress in eloquence is very inconsiderable, in comparison of the advances which we have made in all other parts of learning.

Shall we assert, that the strains of ancient eloquence are unsuitable to our age, and ought not to be imitated by modern orators? Whatever reasons may be made use of to prove this, I am persuaded they will be found, upon examination, to be unsound and unsatisfactory.

First, It may be said, that, in ancient times, during the flourishing period of Greek and Roman learning, the municipal laws, in every state, were but few and simple, and the decision of causes was, in a great measure, left to the equity and common sense of the judges. The study of the laws was not then a laborious occupation, requiring the drudgery of a whole life to finish it, and incompatible with every other study or profession. The great statesmen and generals among the Romans were all lawyers; and Cicero, to show the facility of acquiring this science, declares, that in the midst of all his occupations, he would undertake, in a few days, to make himself a complete civilian.

Now, where a pleader addresses himself to the equity of his judges, he has much more room to display his eloquence, than where he must draw his arguments from strict laws, statutes, and precedents. In the former case many circumstances must be taken in, many personal considerations regarded, and even favour and inclination, which it belongs to the orator, by his art and eloquence, to conciliate, may be disguised under the appearance of equity. But how shall a modern lawyer have leisure to quit his toilsome occupations, in order to gather the flowers of Parnassus? Or what opportunity shall we have of displaying them, amidst the rigid and subtile arguments, objections, and replies, which he is obliged to make use of? The greatest genius, and greatest orator, who should pretend to plead before the *Chancellor*, after a month's study of the laws, would only labour to make himself ridiculous.

I am ready to own, that this circumstance, of the multiplicity and intricacy of laws, is a discouragement to eloquence in modern times; but I assert, that it will not entirely account for the decline of that noble art. It may banish oratory from Westminster Hall, but not from either house of Parliament. Among the Athenians, the Areopagites expressly forbade all allurements of eloquence; and some have pretended, that in the Greek orations, written in the *judiciary* form, there is not so bold and rhetorical a style as appears in the Roman. But to what a pitch did the Athenians carry their eloquence in the *deliberative* kind, when affairs of state were canvassed, and the liberty, happiness, and honour of the republic, were the subject of debate! Disputes of this nature elevate the genius above all others, and give the fullest scope to eloquence; and such disputes are very frequent in this nation.

Secondly, It may be pretended, that the decline of eloquence is owing to the superior good sense of the moderns, who reject with disdain all those rhetorical tricks employed to seduce the judges, and will admit of nothing but solid argument in any debate or deliberation. If a man be accused of murder, the fact must be proved by witnesses and evidence, and the laws will afterwards determine the punishment of the criminal. It would be ridiculous to describe, in strong colours, the horror and cruelty of the action; to introduce the relations of the dead, and, at a signal, make them throw themselves at the feet of the judges, imploring justice, with tears and lamentations: and still more ridiculous would it be, to employ a picture representing the bloody deed, in order to move the judges by the display of so tragical a spectacle, though we know that this artifice was sometimes practised by the pleaders of old. Now, banish the pathetic from public discourses, and you reduce the speakers merely to modern eloquence; that is, to good sense, delivered in proper expressions.

Perhaps it may be acknowledged, that our modern customs, or our superior good sense, if you will, should make our orators more cautious and reserved than the ancient, in attempting to inflame the passions, or elevate the imagination of their audience; but I see no reason why it should make them despair absolutely of succeeding in that attempt. It should make them redouble their art, not abandon it entirely. The ancient orators seem also to have been on their guard against this jealousy of their audience; but they took a different way of eluding it. They hurried away with such a torrent of sublime and pathetic, that they left their hearers no leisure to perceive the artifice by which they were deceived. Nay, to consider the matter aright, they were not deceived by any artifice. The orator, by the force of his own genius and eloquence, first inflamed himself with anger, indignation, pity, sorrow; and then communicated those impetuous movements to his audience.

Does any man pretend to have more good sense than Julius Cæsar?; yet that haughty conqueror, we know, was so subdued by the charms of Cicero's eloquence, that he was, in a manner, constrained to change his settled purpose and resolution, and to absolve a criminal, whom, before that orator pleaded, he was determined to condemn.

Some objections, I own, notwithstanding his vast success, may lie against some passages of the Roman orator. He is too florid and rhetorical: his figures are too striking and palpable: the divisions of his discourse are drawn chiefly from the rules of the schools: and his wit disdains not always the artifice even of a pun, rhyme, or jingle of words. The Grecian addressed himself to an audience much less refined than the Roman senate or judges. The lowest vulgar of Athens were his sovereigns, and the arbiters of his eloquence. Yet is his manner more chaste and austere than that of the other. Could it be copied, its success would be infallible over a modern assembly. It is rapid harmony, exactly adjusted to the sense; it is vehement reasoning, without any appearance of art: it is disdain, anger, boldness, freedom, involved in a continued stream of argument: and, of all human productions, the orations of Demosthenes present to us the models which approach the nearest to perfection.

Thirdly, It may be pretended, that the disorders of the ancient governments, and the enormous crimes of which the citizens were often guilty, afforded much ampler matter for eloquence than can be met with among the moderns. Were there no Verres or Catiline, there would be no Cicero. But that this reason can have no great influence, is evident. It would be easy to find a Philip in modern times, but where shall we find a Demosthenes?

What remains, then, but that we lay the blame on the want of genius, or of judgment, in our speakers, who either found themselves incapable of reaching the heights of ancient eloquence, or rejected all such endeavours, as unsuitable to the spirit of modern assemblies? A few successful attempts of this nature might rouse the genius of the nation, excite the emulation of the youth, and accustom our ears to a more sublime and more pathetic elocution, than what we have been hitherto entertained with. There is certainly something accidental in the first rise and progress of the arts in any nation. I doubt whether a very satisfactory reason can be given why ancient Rome, though it received all its refinements from Greece, could attain only to a relish for statuary, painting, and architecture, without reaching the practice of these arts. While modern Rome has been excited by a few remains found among the ruins of antiquity, and has produced artists of the greatest eminence and distinction. Had such a cultivated genius for oratory, as Waller's for poetry, arisen during the civil wars, when liberty began to be fully established, and popular assemblies to enter into all the most material points of government, I am persuaded so illustrious an example would have given a quite different turn to British eloquence, and made us reach the perfection of the ancient model. Our orators would then have done honour to their country, as well as our poets, geometers, and philosophers; and British Ciceros have appeared, as well as British Archimedeses and Virgils.[26]

---

[26] I have confessed that there is something accidental in the origin and progress of the arts in any nation; and yet I cannot forbear thinking, that if the other learned and polite nations of Europe had possessed the same advantages of a popular government, they would probably have carried eloquence to a greater height than it has yet reached in Britain. The French sermons, especially those of Flechier and Bourdaloue, are much superior to the English in this particular; and in Flechier there are many strokes of the most sublime poetry. His funeral sermon on the Marechal de Turenne, is a good instance. None but private causes in that country, are ever debated before their Parliament or Courts of Judicature; but, notwithstanding this disadvantage, there appears a spirit of eloquence in many of their lawyers, which, with proper cultivation and encouragement, might rise to the greatest heights. The pleadings of Patru are very elegant, and give us room to imagine what so fine a genius could have performed in questions concerning public liberty or slavery, peace or war, who exerts himself with such success in debates concerning the price of an old horse, or the gossiping story of a quarrel betwixt an abbess and her nuns. For it is remarkable, that this polite writer, though esteemed by all the men of wit in his time, was never employed in the most considerable causes of their courts of judicature, but lived and died in poverty; from an ancient prejudice industriously propagated by the Dunces in all countries, *That a man of genius is unfit for business*. The disorders produced by the ministry of Cardinal Mazarine, made the Parliament of Paris enter into the discussion of public affairs; and during that short interval, there appeared many symptoms of the revival of ancient eloquence. The Avocat-General, Talon, in an oration, invoked on his knees the spirit of St Louis to look down with compassion on his divided and unhappy people, and to inspire them, from above, with the love of concord and unanimity. The members of the French Academy have attempted to give us models of eloquence in their harangues at their admittance; but having no subject to discourse upon, they have run altogether into a fulsome strain of panegyric and flattery, the most barren of all subjects. Their style, however, is commonly, on these occasions, very elevated and sublime, and might reach the greatest heights, were it employed on a subject more favourable and engaging.

It is seldom or never found, when a false taste in poetry or eloquence prevails among any people, that it has been preferred to a true, upon comparison and reflection. It commonly prevails merely from ignorance of the true, and from the want of perfect models to lead men into a juster apprehension, and more refined relish of those productions of genius. When *these* appear, they soon unite all suffrages in their favour, and, by their natural and powerful charms, gain over even the most prejudiced to the love and admiration of them. The principles of every passion, and of every sentiment, is in every man; and, when touched properly, they rise to life, and warm the heart, and convey that satisfaction, by which a work of genius is distinguished from the adulterate beauties of a capricious wit and fancy. And, if this observation be true, with regard to all the liberal arts, it must be peculiarly so

---

There are some circumstances in the English temper and genius, which are disadvantageous to the progress of eloquence, and render all attempts of that kind more dangerous and difficult among them, than among any other nation in the universe. The English are conspicuous for good sense, which makes them very jealous of any attempts to deceive them, by the flowers of rhetoric and elocution. They are also peculiarly *modest*; which makes them consider it as a piece of arrogance to offer any thing but reason to public assemblies, or attempt to guide them by passion or fancy. I may, perhaps, be allowed to add that the people in general are not remarkable for delicacy of taste, or for sensibility to the charms of the Muses. Their musical parts, to use the expression of a noble author, are but indifferent. Hence their comic poets, to move them, must have recourse to obscenity; their tragic poets to blood and slaughter. And hence, their orators, being deprived of any such resource, have abandoned altogether the hopes of moving them, and have confined themselves to plain argument and reasoning.

These circumstances, joined to particular accidents, may, perhaps, have retarded the growth of eloquence in this kingdom; but will not be able to prevent its success, if ever it appear amongst us. And one may safely pronounce, that this is a field in which the most flourishing laurels may yet be gathered, if any youth of accomplished genius, thoroughly acquainted with all the polite arts, and not ignorant of public business, should appear in Parliament, and accustom our ears to an eloquence more commanding and pathetic. And to confirm me in this opinion, there occur two considerations, the one derived from ancient, the other from modern times.

with regard to eloquence; which, being merely calculated for the public, and for men of the world, cannot, without any pretence of reason, appeal from the people to more refined judges, but must submit to the public verdict without reserve or limitation. Whoever, upon comparison, is deemed by a common audience the greatest orator, ought most certainly to be pronounced such by men of science and erudition. And though an indifferent speaker may triumph for a long time, and be esteemed altogether perfect by the vulgar, who are satisfied with his accomplishments, and know not in what he is defective; yet, whenever the true genius arises, he draws to him the attention of every one, and immediately appears superior to his rival.

Now, to judge by this rule, ancient eloquence, that is, the sublime and passionate, is of a much juster taste than the modern, or the argumentative and rational, and, if properly executed, will always have more command and authority over mankind. We are satisfied with our mediocrity, because we have had no experience of any thing better: but the ancients had experience of both; and upon comparison, gave the preference to that kind of which they have left us such applauded models. For, if I mistake not, our modern eloquence is of the same style or species with that which ancient critics denominated Attic eloquence, that is, calm, elegant, and subtile, which instructed the reason more than affected the passions, and never raised its tone above argument or common discourse. Such was the eloquence of Lysias among the Athenians, and of Calvus among the Romans. These were esteemed in their time; but, when compared with Demosthenes and Cicero, were eclipsed like a taper when set in the rays of a meridian sun. Those latter orators possessed the same elegance, and subtilty, and force of argument with the former; but, what rendered them chiefly admirable, was that pathetic and sublime, which, on proper occasions, they threw into their discourse, and by which they commanded the resolution of their audience.

Of this species of eloquence we have scarcely had any instance in England, at least in our public speakers. In our writers, we have had some instances which have met with great applause, and might assure our ambitious youth of equal or superior glory in attempts for the revival of ancient eloquence. Lord Bolingbroke's productions, with all their defects in argument, method, and precision, contain a force and energy which our orators scarcely ever aim at; though it is evident that such an elevated style has much better grace in a speaker than in a writer, and is assured of more prompt and more astonishing success. It is there seconded by the graces of voice and action: the movements are mutually communicated between the orator and the audience: and the very aspect of a large assembly, attentive to the discourse of one man, must inspire him with a peculiar elevation, sufficient to give a propriety to the strongest figures and expressions. It is true, there is a great prejudice against *set speeches*; and a man cannot escape ridicule, who repeats a discourse as a schoolboy does his lesson, and takes no notice of any thing that has been advanced in the course of the debate. But where is the necessity of falling into this absurdity? A public speaker must know beforehand the question under debate. He may compose all the arguments, objections, and answers, such as he thinks will be most proper for his discourse. If any thing new occur, he may supply it from his own invention; nor will the difference be very apparent between his elaborate and his extemporary compositions. The mind naturally continues with the same *impetus* or *force*, which it has acquired by its motion as a vessel, once impelled by the oars, carries on its course for some time when the original impulse is suspended.

I shall conclude this subject with observing, that, even though our modern orators should not elevate their style, or aspire to a rivalship with the ancient; yet there is, in most of their speeches, a material defect which they might correct, without departing from that composed air of argument and reasoning to which they limit their ambition. Their great affectation of extemporary discourses has made them reject all order and method, which seems so requisite to argument, and without which it is scarcely possible to produce an entire conviction on the mind. It is not that one would recommend many divisions in a public discourse, unless the subject very evidently offer them: but it is easy, without this formality, to observe a method, and make that method conspicuous to the hearers, who will be infinitely pleased to see the arguments rise naturally from one another, and will retain a more thorough persuasion than can arise from the strongest reasons which are thrown together in confusion.

www.ingramcontent.com/pod-product-compliance
Lightning Source LLC
Chambersburg PA
CBHW071737090426
42738CB00011B/2507